HOW TO PUBLISH AND MARKET YOUR FAMILY HISTORY

FOURTH EDITION
by
CARL BOYER, 3rd

CARL BOYER, 3rd
SANTA CLARITA, CALIFORNIA
1993

LIBRARY OF CONGRESS CATALOG CARD NUMBER: 92-97111

ISBN 0-936124-16-4

CARL BOYER, 3rd
P. O. BOX 333
SANTA CLARITA, CALIFORNIA 91322-0333

CONTENTS

PREFACE

On the day when the preface to the original edition of this work was written, in 1982, the undersigned received a copy of the review in the *New York Genealogical and Biographical Record* of *Ancestral Lines Revised*: "The original edition of Mr. Boyer's *Ancestral Lines* and his *Slade-Babcock Genealogy* were universally praised by editors of genealogical magazines. The revision incorporates the material in the two previous books, presenting genealogies of all of the related families down to the point where a female descendant married into another of the families studied, at which point she rates an asterisk.

"Each family history is minutely documented, keyed to a 46-page bibliography. As in his previous books, Mr. Boyer analyzes carefully sources he considers of doubtful value, and especially conflicting statements. The book is a model of how information on many ancestral families should be presented and documented."

This volume is intended to show how to publish a family history, regardless of the number of families involved, in a way allowing the author-publisher to achieve critical acclaim as well as a limited taxable profit.

This compiler has no doubt that this work will prove to be useful to many genealogists, particularly those with little experience. However, the reader should understand the intention in writing this book. First, the original edition was published at a time a commercial success was needed, so that even in a time of recession it would be possible, financially, to continue to have some time free to work on genealogical studies which would take a considerable amount of time, once published, to recoup the investment involved. Second, as the compiler's previous work had been seen by many as a model, and thus there was a demand for appearances as a speaker with the resulting questions from both audiences and correspondents, it seemed worthwhile to attempt to put together a helpful volume.

Once it was decided to do the book a careful outline was made. As the chapters were written the drafts were checked against the outline to assure that the organization would be as originally planned. Nonetheless, two problems were perceived. One was that the systems approach to publishing is so complex, interweaving philosophy, scope, marketing and a multitude of other facets of producing any book, that some readers would find it very difficult to understand. The other was that readers may find some questions remained unanswered.

The first two editions did not present great problems to readers, however, if the letters resulting from them were a fair indication.

Nonetheless, the third edition was revised in those areas which resulted in questions from the public as well as from a normal turn of events.

This fourth edition, also revised to reflect recent changes in the publishing industry, will be the object of a single printing so that the next edition can respond to the questions and criticism generated. With the text now on computer disk, ensuing editions will come easily.

The reader should not be concerned about being far enough along in his research to be ready to publish. The genealogist who needs to read this book the most is the beginner. The desire to publish must be the foundation upon which a research project is built. As will be seen in the text, the failure to publish is the failure to preserve the family's history. Research must be organized, not aimless, and must be of a quality worth publication if it is to be meaningful.

It is true that some, if not all too many, are content to peruse the literature, tie their ancestors to distant branches, claim a few royal lines (often long disproved) and recite their tales to all who will listen. However, many beginning family historians are truly interested in preserving tradition and researching the history behind this tradition, even if it means that some of the oral heritage must be cast aside as inaccurate or fabricated. Hopefully this book will assist those who are interested in doing scholarly work, and will discourage some who are not. Certainly there are enough scholars in the field today that it is becoming increasingly difficult to publish a poor work without arousing negative reviews.

Acknowledgements and thanks are due to a few readers of the first edition. John F. Elsbree of 56 Brooks Street, Brighton, MA 02135, raised a number of questions and contributed a list of errors in spelling, syntax, and the like. Charles W. True, Jr., of 9324 McFall Drive, El Paso, TX 79925, raised helpful points about copyright and libel. Thelma F. Prince of 44 Clemson Road, Parlin, NJ 08859, wrote concerning comparative costs and the additional benefits of working with Gateway Press. Mrs. M. B. (Opal) Lousin of 5338 West Hutchinson, Chicago, IL 60641, listed some errors and raised excellent points concerning whether the numbering system could be understood by those who might not read an author's preface. Sidney D. Smith, P. O. Box 366, Harbert, MI 49115, sent excellent examples of his mailings requesting information from relatives; they were not used in this book because of their great length, but they are quite irresistible. Also a big thank you is due to those who have continued to mail copies of their advertising flyers with a note about how they had completed their books. Those notes have provided a big lift.

Those readers who have found this title in a library will receive information on how to order a personal copy if they will drop a note to the undersigned, who tries to answer such queries, as well as orders, by return mail. Delays of a few weeks may occur only when this compiler is leading groups on foreign tours.

Regretfully, it is likely that other correspondence will not enjoy such prompt treatment, as in addition to teaching full time, doing research and running a publishing business, I am presently serving as a member of the City Council of Santa Clarita, the largest new city formed in the history of humankind. Indeed, publication of this volume was delayed considerably due to the time required to serve a term as Mayor from mid-December 1990.

Carl Boyer, 3rd
P. O. Box 333
Santa Clarita, California 91322

22 September 1992

THE DECISION TO PUBLISH

The first decision that you must make, once you have decided to undertake genealogical research, is to publish the results of that work. Publication is compelled by the very nature of the task, which depends upon the cooperation and support of many members of the family, most of whom have little real interest in preserving records. Therefore, your relatives must be given some reason to make an effort to contribute to the project at hand. Furthermore, once the decision to publish has been made, the writer will become aware of the acute need for high standards of scholarship and an orderly approach to problems.

Research into family history must not be taken lightly. In the beginning stages few people realize the magnitude of the enterprise. After all, many can put down on paper what they know of their ancestry in a few minutes, on a couple of pages. It is too easy to assume that a little work will reveal all there is to know, and that the required effort to organize this information into a book will take little more than a shuffling of data into an understandable format and a few hours of typing.

It does not appear that people are born to be genealogists. Indeed, many family historians are simply folk who developed from having a healthy interest in the history of their environment into having a desire to know what part their own people played in its development. You must consider philosophically your reasons for wanting to write the record of your family, for without a sound reason for doing the job you are likely to do it poorly.

The worst genealogist is the person who seeks reflected glory, ties to well known figures or royal ancestry. That is not to say that someone seeking membership in the Sons or Daughters of the American Revolution should not undertake to prove their eligibility, but rather to make the point that one must be willing to accept the facts as they exist rather than fabricating a relationship simply to prove something of significance to their own outlook.

It is important for a person to be comfortable with oneself, to be accepting of one's "station" in life, so to speak, so that the bad can be taken with the good. It is true that, as you gain acquaintance with hundreds of ancestors, you are likely to find rather a mixed lot, even if the proverbial horse thief may be the most elusive of all. This writer has found accused witches, corrupt politicians, adulterous triangles which would make soap opera scriptwriters blush, as well as renegades and wife beaters among his relatives, but, after all, these people were human, and often amusing in a way. Others proved not to be as bad as some had made them out to be, once a thorough investigation of the facts had been completed. One thread which often runs through the family is that of public service, if only because in the early years of our nation there were few people and many offices, but for every politician who took advantage of his position there were many who served well.

An interest in genealogy may be awakened in many different ways. If the reader will forgive the writer telling something about himself, it may prove instructive. By the time this writer was twelve years old he was aware that an aging edition of *American Boyers* had long been gathering dust on the bookshelves in the living room of the family home in Wallingford, Pennsylvania. The book simply sat there, unused, for many years. Then, in the eighth grade, a traditional history unit on the Civil War was presented by the teacher, Carl E. Kane. When this young student mentioned it to his father it was time to bring out the old letters which Samuel Dodge Boyer had written home from the front. These eighty-eight year old papers proved mildly interesting to a thirteen year old, so he made a copy of one to take to his teacher.

He was to learn later that many of his classmates were descendants, as he was, from families which had lived in Pennsylvania for over two hundred and sixty years. However, none of them knew of their ancestors' participation in the Civil War, so the copy of a great-great-grandfather's letter was of real interest to the class. It is not recalled whether any extra credit was awarded for bringing in the letter, but Mr. Kane was never short of kind words, at least, for a student who had shown a little extra interest in history. In any event, this young man went home to blow the dust off the old family book.

It was really quite fascinating, reading the introduction describing the Boii tribe which had fought Julius Caesar and lost in 58 B.C. The story of their subsequent migration to Bohemia and Bavaria, and mention of many distinguished members of the Bayer, Beyer and Boyer families from a number of countries, all within three pages, served to kindle a spark of interest.

Then it was discovered that little slips of paper in the book marked the generations from John Philip Beyer, an immigrant to Pennsylvania about 1738, to one's father, whose birth in 1908 was mentioned. This was all in Chapter 3, which was really not so interesting as it consisted of little more than data, names and dates with a few places mentioned here and there, with just a few lines of biographical detail on occasion. They all seemed to be "just a bunch of farmers," but the eighth grader's father said that that was not true, that one had spent many years in a penitentiary! Closer examination proved this to be true, even if the time had been spent as a paid member of the staff, as librarian.

Four years then passed before any further thought was given to the story of the family. In August of 1955 a large number of the family gathered for Grandfather's funeral. Granddad was a man who was close to his grandchildren, who in turn had enjoyed living closely enough to their grandparents and all their aunts and uncles that they knew them well, with the exception of Mother's father, an older man who had died shortly after his first grandchild was born. Nonetheless, those of the younger generation were not aware that there were so many other relatives, including cousin Townsend.

In 1955 Townsend Harding Boyer was seventy-one. He had been interested in the family history for much of his life, and had served as President of the Association of American Boyers more than thirty years before. Following the ceremony it happened that Townsend singled out a seventeen-year-old as possibly having a willing ear, and began spinning yarns of the Boyers, the Dodges, and Titus Evans, the latter an old Welsh printer who had been "kicked out of his homeland for having published an illicit edition of the Bible."

As the family gathering broke up, Townsend extended an invitation to visit him in Haddonfield, New Jersey, a town perhaps twenty miles from Wallingford, which this student had never seen. There had been frequent trips across New Jersey, driving to New Hampshire, and one trip to Cape May to visit a friend who was working there for the summer, and even a few to Wildwood and Ocean City, but none to Haddonfield.

If Dad were asked today, no doubt he would not recall whether he was interested in seeing Townsend again, or whether he was afraid his son would get lost on the drive, but in any event, when the time came to take a ferry across the Delaware, there were two visitors. The younger one carried a small notebook, and years later was so glad that he had, and had taken copious notes the whole time Townsend talked.

That Saturday in September Townsend told basically the same stories, the difference being that this time he showed his copy of Theron Royal Woodward's *Dodge Genealogy: Descendants of Tristram Dodge*, notes from an article in *The New York Genealogical and Biographical Record* concerning a relationship with John Jacob Astor, and a catalog from Goodspeed's Book Shop in Boston. While Townsend spoke the pages of the notebook were filled with biography, bibliographical data (how helpful those dreadful term papers in high school had proved to be!), and Goodspeed's address.

Some weeks later an inquiry went off to Boston about a new catalog and a copy of Woodward's book, both of which were purchased. However, these were soon retired to a shelf, for it was time to go to college, and the family history had to be put aside once again.

Seven years later, after wandering from Pennsylvania to colleges in Tennessee, Scotland, Texas and Ohio, having earned two degrees and completed two years of teaching, this writer married. As a young wife married to a poverty-stricken school teacher, Chris continued working, and although the young couple and her parents all lived in Cincinnati, the topic of family history never seemed to come up until shortly before the young couple moved to Los Angeles. The conversation had turned to the trips Chris had made with her family to New York State as a child, her relatives in Troy, and some of the family legends. Soon the young history teacher had volunteered to do some research, if only he could be given some notes to get him started.

Teaching at San Fernando High School did not allow much leisure. There were new courses to teach and lesson plans to develop, and a child on the way. More graduate work was undertaken and an adult school assignment followed, but in 1964 a Saturday was taken for a visit to the Los Angeles Public Library, which, it had been learned, had a genealogy room. Eureka! The mass of family and county histories and vital records available in print was incredible.

A search for Chris' ancestors, "Peter Babcock" and "John Slade," was quickly rewarded, except that the data in print did not seem to match the family notes very well. This proved to be a fine lesson for the genealogist, for having no sense of attempting to prove anything about these families, he was content with digging for the truth.

Some data was copied and a section of one book was photostated. Over the next week the notes were organized into chart form and the results were sent to Cincinnati. Then, and only then, did it become apparent that it might be helpful to do some reading in genealogical research method! Unfortunately, in the early work done on these lines the task of noting bibliographical details on each photostat was neglected, so that much of the work had to be repeated. How many have made that mistake!

The letters to Cincinnati resulted in correspondence coming from all over the East. Chris' mother had copied data for her brothers and sisters. From there word of the modest success of that Saturday's work had spread to cousins and a genealogist in North Troy, Frances D. Broderick, who had suggested that she might be able to help on a professional basis, albeit at very modest rates.

Soon Mrs. Broderick and some of the relatives were sending material which showed that the Peter Babcock and John Slade of family tradition were in reality "Honest" John Babcock and his son-in-law, Benjamin Slade. There were so many requests for copies of the research results that the work of typing carbons was becoming exhausting, particularly as many corrections were being made and numerous revisions and extensions of lines were being developed. Copying facilities were not readily available once a move had been made to Newhall in 1969. Thus, *Slade-Babcock Genealogy* was born out of necessity. The promise of a book in preparation helped the members of the family to wait patiently.

Nonetheless the practice of making some carbons continued, thankfully, for in spite of studying method it took Betty Ambrose of Knoxville, Tennessee, to point out that a William Slade could not have come to Rhode Island in 1639 and died ninety years later, aged sixty-seven! From that point on, all data was checked for illogical chronology. John F. Elsbree of Brighton, Massachusetts, has written of a book containing mention of a lady widowed in 1583 who had children by her second husband as late as 1626, and of a bride who was married in the same place, and on the same date, as her parents!

More books on method were purchased and read. While each volume covered much the same material, the ideas were presented in different ways, with a variety of examples, and soon they were being retained with the result that research became more efficient. Applications for membership in a few societies were filled out, books were borrowed by mail, and other library facilities were being discovered. Colleges and universities proved to be helpful, for while their collections did not contain many genealogies, they did include topography, local history, collections of colonial newspapers on microfiche cards, atlases, maps and gazetteers.

By 1967 it was impossible to put the project aside. No longer could a book be put back on the shelf to be forgotten for a year or two. There were simply too many letters contributing information, providing encouragement, expressing thanks, and asking questions. Publication of a book, however, was obviously still some years away, and funds for the project were running short. There were three children in the family now.

It seemed that some interim method of publication might be in order, so the *Slade-Babcock Genealogical Newsletter* was born and about sixty subscriptions were sold. These funds helped, for the newsletter, which ran from six to over thirty pages an issue six times a year, was duplicated on a ditto machine and was inexpensive to produce and mail. This medium elicited more help from genealogists interested in the early Slade and Babcock families, if not more closely related, and more material was contributed. The most valuable aspect of publishing articles at the time, however, was that their appearance was met with critical mail, pointing out errors and raising questions. Criticism, well meant and well taken, is very helpful.

The newsletter was not meant as a work to be bound and saved, though some libraries subscribed once it was advertized in *The Genealogical Helper*. All contributions were printed (some with editorial notes) as they came in the mail, the masters having been typed as the material arrived. When the deadline for duplicating approached, whatever number of pages there were made up that issue.

Meanwhile another little publication, also done on a spirit duplicator, saw the light of day. *The Ancestry and Descendants of Abram Ludwig Boyer and Sarah Dodge* enjoyed, mercifully, very limited circulation. As work on the Boyer and Dodge families had progressed at a slower rate, while the Slade and Babcock families received most of the effort because the members of the latter families were more interested and supportive, it became apparent that the newsletter method of encouraging criticism was an important part of the learning process concerning genealogical writing and publishing, and that the Boyer-Dodge work should never have been duplicated. While the lines were substantially correct, there were many errors in specific data, and the word "cemetery" had been misspelled "cemetary" numerous times.

The work load grew. Soon there were fifty-four surnames to be researched and verified for publication in the Slade-Babcock book. Perhaps it was fortunate for the project that there had been little attention paid in the early stages to the fact that the number of ancestors doubles each generation, and the number of descendants can grow at a much faster pace. Fourth cousins were being found just a few blocks away, and more distant relatives on the street where we lived.

By 1969 it was taking hours of work to unearth each new tiny bit of data on the ancestry. Many of the descendants' lines had been charted, with addresses appended, and although at that time no deadline had been set it was clear that it was time to put form letters and questionnaires into the mail to all known members of the family. By this time the effort had been going on for five years and the project was well known to the second and third cousins.

The newsletter was allowed to lapse, no subscriptions for a third year of publication having been solicited, and the final issue contained notice that it would be the last. It was time to type "final drafts" of the material on the ancestry of Benjamin and Angeline (Babcock) Slade, and concentrate on their descendants. Each of their children had at least one living descendant who was willing to help. As the decision to establish a deadline was made only two living members of the family had not responded to repeated letters in time for publication of their children's data, and one line was lost.

The lost line involved a situation in which a young man had married, been killed in a railroad accident, and left a child born posthumously. His widow had remarried, the child adopted by her second husband, and contact with the family had been lost. Fortunately someone remembered the name of a brother of the widow, and said he might still be living in Lincoln, Nebraska. Within three minutes of receiving this information in a letter, the phone number of a person of the same name was obtained from information in Lincoln. The brother answered the phone on the first try, answered a number of questions and promised to respond to more questions to be sent in the mail. He was so helpful that the line was developed by the deadline. Curiously enough, of the two who did not send data on their children in time for publication, one responded in time for them to be included in a supplement, and the other, who never sent the data, bought three copies of the book, one for himself and one each for two sons never to be identified by more than their first names.

Meanwhile this writer was becoming more sophisticated about the art of publishing, due to a fortuitous circumstance. One evening in adult school class he parried a student's remark about teachers looking forward to a long summer vacation with the comment that vacation, for a teacher, meant a long, hungry summer of unemployment with no paychecks. At the conclusion of the next session one of the ladies in the class suggested going to apply for an office job with the printing firm where her husband worked. There followed three successive summers of low paid but instructive employment in estimating the cost of printing jobs, typing invoices, mailing statements, doing quarterly tax returns and all the other tasks that a general office employee in a small firm must do. Not only did he learn how to conduct a small business, but there was plenty of time to ask questions about the technical aspects of publishing. This led to a decision to treat the project as a business, keeping accurate records of expenses and income for tax purposes.

Thus a series of conversations, letters and experiences had helped to shape the structure and content of *Slade-Babcock Genealogy*, but all this had taken several years. There is no need for others to learn by accident, by inspiration, or dumb luck. One need only take some good advice from one who has learned the hard way.

Let us return to the problem of the format of a successful family history, which includes the questions of structure and content. In short, what should be the scope?

Probably the least desirable thing to plan is a book which is about all of one's own ancestors and nothing else. The major problem is that there will be only one customer for such a tome, oneself. In the case of Slade-Babcock it so happened that the surname of most immediate concern to the closest relatives was Marshall, but the Marshall ancestry was hard to trace, more was known about the Slade and Babcock lines, and the Slade cousins were interested. Indeed, one cousin, Jim Breslin of Vermont, sent numerous letters and photographs of and about the Slade and Babcock families. He also provided a number of addresses of people in the branches who contributed much data once they learned of plans to publish.

Thus the people interested in helping and the ease of tracing only the Slade and Babcock lines had dictated that the book deal only with the ancestors and descendants of one couple, each of whom had been born shortly after 1800. While "Slade-Babcock Genealogy" had proved a satisfactory working title, someone had pleaded that the full title be as full and descriptive as possible, pointing out that Library of Congress catalog cards and periodicals will often list a full title but give little other information. The more descriptive the title, the more likely people are to believe the book may be helpful. Then they will buy the book. Thus the full title became *Slade-Babcock Genealogy: Ancestors and Descendants of Benjamin and Angeline (Babcock) Slade of Rensselaer and Saratoga Counties, New York.* It was tempting to include even more, perhaps adding "including the Anthony, Chase, Coggeshall, Holmes, Jenckes, Read, Sherman and Forty-five Allied Families." A few more sales might have resulted from bibliographical entries, but it was deemed unwise to emulate John Camden Hotten, whose famous book is most often simply called "Persons" because the length of the title is beyond reason.

Once structure and content had been decided, the questions of style, accuracy and organization remained. The reading of numerous works in the literature of genealogy makes one realize that much nineteenth-century material was written in a flowery, puffed, self-indulgent style. Sometimes it was done so poorly that one has great difficulty figuring out what was meant. Altogether the greatest problem tended to be pronouns which failed to refer back to the proper antecedents. Some of the twentieth-century pieces are not much better, but as most of the members of the Slade and Babcock families had lived in New York or New England, this researcher had the good fortune of getting into the habit of reading *The New York Genealogical and Biographical Record* and *The New England Historical and Genealogical Register* from cover to cover. It soon became apparent that a formal style, written in careful English, would be truly clear. Even more helpful, though not so much in the matter of style, was *The American Genealogist*, in which critical analysis of problems abounds.

Here a few words of encouragement may be in order for those whose ancestors did not come over with Capt. John Smith or on the *Mayflower*.

Perhaps the immigrants came to America to escape the pogroms in Russia. Perhaps they were brought over on slave ships. Perhaps they "met the boat." In such cases written records may be quite inadequate. Publication of a fine genealogy does not necessarily involve bulk or the tracing of many generations and many different family lines. Whether a family may be political refugees or pioneers in the Old Southwest, lines may be difficult to work. The important consideration in any event is that of structure and content, and some will do very well to trace their ancestry to the immigrants and no further, or merely to the first settlers of a western town. In such cases it is wise to preserve family tradition as quickly as possible, before more of it is lost in the passing of generations. One must then concentrate on the descendants, perhaps filling out the record of the past with historical explanations of the circumstances of people like the ancestors.

Once tradition has been preserved there will always be a chance that future generations will have the opportunity to search appropriate records not now available to the public in any form, but when tradition is lost the link to the past may be gone forever. Not only is there never a day to waste in preserving tradition, a fact most genealogists recognize, but one who procrastinates about getting one's work into print stands the chance that this work will be lost forever once one is not around to treasure it. This point must be considered seriously.

Much of the narrative above points to the fact that most genealogists learn by trial and error. Rules and procedures become apparent as one works and reworks ancestral lines. Some rules, observed carefully from the beginning, will save the researcher much grief.

First, one must always mark each Xerox copy or note with bibliographical data. Photocopies should be checked as they are made to see that important headings, page numbers or some lines of text are not missing. Unfortunately, some are too fussy in this regard, standing at the machine no matter how many people are in line, carefully checking each copy before making the next one. Sloppy copying can be a source of great inconvenience. Consider the time, energy and expense involved in repeated unnecessary trips to the library to check for sources, page numbers and missing text. When this writer did his graduate research in history he was most careful, perhaps because his papers were graded or subject to criticism from his professors and fellow students.

Perhaps incredibly, all these good habits disappeared when genealogical research began, probably because initially there was no plan to publish.

Determining the source of a Xeroxed page can be a horrendous task. Fortunately a collection of index volumes as well as other genealogists at a library can be most helpful. Experienced librarians and researchers can often identify a book or periodical simply by a quick look at type style and content. Cindy Lo Buglio, an expert on Latin American genealogy, has told for publication the story of her first notes on Jose Sepúlveda as being marked "from the 'Red Book'." Sadly, when she finally went looking for the complete publication data she could no longer find the book; it must have been rebound!

The second rule at the elementary level is to check every bit of data for logic. The problem of illogical chronology has been illustrated above in the case of William Slade. As it turned out, there were two William Slades, father and son, but the original error had been copied blissfully from a genealogy which proved, in most other respects, to be fairly accurate. Location should not be ignored either. If the place name does not seem right, the data probably refers to another person of the same name. Of course even if the place is correct there may be problems. This compiler's most difficult problem involves determining the ancestry of the John Brown who married Lydia Bullock in Rehoboth, Massachusetts, in 1762. Not only were there several John Browns in or near Rehoboth at the time, but three of them married girls named Lydia!

Third, check every source listed in family histories to see if the material was copied accurately. Errors abound, and even if the manuscript text was perfect there may be typographical errors made by a typist or typesetter. Proof reading a family history is most difficult. Thus many will publish typed material to avoid printers' errors. However, some have not only miscopied, but have incorrectly altered such data as the "tenth month" to read October even when the calendar generally in use at the time clearly meant December as the month in question. In most cases it is best to copy a record as it stands, spelling the month out in brackets if one can determine which month was meant without doubt. As an example, Thomas Potter was born in North Kingston, Rhode Island, on "8 11th month [Feb.] 1695/6," 1695 being the year given in the original record, when the year began on the 25th day of March, and 1696 corresponding to the year as it would have been stated had our current calendar been in use at that time.

No researcher should begin working in older or foreign records without a thorough understanding of the problems created by the use of various calendars. A number of methods manuals are very helpful in achieving this. In colonial America calendar usage varied from one province to the next, and even from one clerk to another. One cannot be sure which calendar was in use, in many cases, without looking over at least a full year of the record in question to see, for example, when the year began.

Research can be hampered by the fact that many sources are not available to a particular genealogist at any given time. Some records are no longer extant, having been lost in a fire at a town clerk's home or at the county courthouse, or having suffered deterioration from storage in a damp basement. Other data is in the hands of uncooperative bureaucrats, perhaps made cranky by an army of overbearing genealogists who have made unreasonable demands. Not even the Library of Congress has copies of all printed materials. Gravestones have weathered beyond reading, been stolen, or have sunk into the ground, location unknown.

However, many sources can be found with reasonable effort. In some cases correspondents working on the same lines can verify records they have checked already. Many archivists and others who care for records are a joy with whom to work, and will make an effort to please the considerate researcher far beyond the level of service one might expect. If the researcher is well prepared, with his own records at hand and with a list of concise questions, he can expect a better reception and more cooperation.

Those not having access to large libraries may be frustrated because of the time it takes to borrow just a few books on inter-library loan or by mail from societies one has joined. However, if you are canvassing descendants for data at the same time, progress can be made. It must not be forgotten, from the beginning, that when one eventually goes into print any sloppy work will be noted by reviewers, while good work merits comments very helpful to sales. Every care must always be taken to preserve your reputation as a thorough researcher.

In some cases you will find that the source did not contain the material at all. As for the writers of other works, all too many were willing to fabricate pedigrees, merrily lying about their sources as they went along. Others simply speculated, and, in the following section quoted from *Ancestral Lines Revised*, this compiler's introduction to the Babcock family, you can see how one such problem was handled by this writer.

"According to Stephen Babcock's *Babcock Genealogy* (1903), the *Dictionary of American Family Antiquity* has described the Babcock coat of arms: 'He beareth Argent; three pale cocks on a Fesse cotised, gules. Crest, a cock's head. Motto, Deus spes mea.' Thus the coat of arms is a silver shield with three pale cocks emblazoned on a broad red band, crossing the shield horizontally, with a narrow red band on each side of it; with a cock's head above the shield and the motto 'God Is My Hope' below.

"This coat of arms may not be borne legally by any of the Babcocks listed below, because their ancestry cannot be traced to the original bearer, and it is thus only of academic interest. It appears to be a composite of several coats of arms of the same general family. There were four different coats of arms worn by different English Badcocks, as they spell the name to this day. These branches of the family were located in St. Winow, Cornwall, in Essex and Middlesex, in Devonshire, and in Lincolnshire and Buckinghamshire, where the fourth was borne by a Lt. Col. Lovell Benjamin Badcock.

"Hotten's *Persons* mentioned a William Badcocke from St. Hillary in Cornwall, who sailed in the *Margarett* from Plymouth, England, for St. Christopher's in the British West Indies in 1633.

"The Badcock family name is of English or Saxon origin, at the least quite old, with some dating it back to 449 A.D. [*Dict. Am. Fam. Ant.*, 3:199], if one can believe such claims. Hinman [*Puritan Settlers*, 92, 106] stated that James[1] Badcock, the early immigrant from England to Rhode Island, was a younger brother of Richard Badcock, a knight whose family had lived in the same mansion in Wivenhoe, county Essex, for nineteen generations, thus dating the family back to the time of the Norman invasion in 1066. Hinman cited Wright's *History of Essex*, which was supposed to contain a record of a visitation made by Sir William Seager in 1612, as well as of the Badcock mansion standing then and as late as 1850.

"Tales of long family trees are often fabricated out of wishful thinking, where an inexperienced researcher confuses lines and is drawn into a wrong branch about which data is plentiful, but Hinman was not merely confused, for the fact is that there is no Badcock pedigree in Wright's work. Granted, he may have been misled by an English genealogist attempting to please an unsuspecting client. This compiler has searched every page of Thomas Wright's *The History and Typography of the County of Essex*, 2 volumes [London: George Virtue, 1836, iv, viii, 692+836], and found not one mention of the name of Badcock or Babcock not listed in the index, with those being listed as place names rather than as names of persons.

"Correspondence with the British Museum revealed that one other edition of Wright's work does exist. Arthur H. Noble, an officer of the Society of Genealogists, London, was kind enough to investigate: 'The earlier is undated but the frontispiece is an engraving dated 1833. The catalogue gives the date as 1835. The second edition is larger. The index of the first edition has no Badcock. I read through the section on Wivenhoe but there is no mention of Badcock.' Mr. Noble wrote to the Archivist of the Essex Record Office, who replied, 'An examination of the most likely sources has failed to reveal any mention of the Badcock family of Wivenhoe. The incumbent at Wivenhoe has in his custody all the registers from 1560 and a transcript of the years 1560-1688.' This incumbent did not reply to a letter from Mr. Noble.

"Mr. Noble continued, 'I looked through Boyd's marriage index. Wivenhoe marriages from 1560 to 1754 are included but there are no Badcocks. There are over 50 Badcock marriages in other parts of Essex between 1588 and 1750 after which the family seems to have dwindled.'

"Mr. Noble went on to mention other Badcocks: John Badcock, tailor of Colchester in the seventeenth century mentioned in the Victoria County History of Essex, also families in Cornwall, mostly at Bodmin, in the files of the Society of Genealogists. In the document files there was mention of Abraham Badcock, born Barnstaple 13 June 1749, who had a brother Daniel of Bampton who 'made a fortune in America' and bought an estate at Combehead Dulverton. There were four generations in this pedigree and the third was General Sir Alexander Robert Badcock, who died in 1807. Abraham had died in 1747. There was a will of Lovell Badcock, dated 14 July 1749, who had lands in Lincolnshire and Buckinghamshire, and sons Lovell and Thomas Stanhope. "A look at the Badcocks in the indices of the Prerogative Court of Canterbury, from 1600 to 1700, revealed a few, but none in Essex. 'There might be wills in the Essex Consistory and Archdeaconry Courts and this would involve quite a search.'

"Concerning the manor of Badcocks in East Thorp, mentioned by Wright, 'I have looked up East Thorp in some old gazeteers but it is not there. Nor is there a parish of East Thorpe. I think it must be a part of Thorp le Soken, a parish about 12 miles east of Colchester and not far from Wivenhoe.'

"Babcock descendants are indebted to Mr. Noble, who gave freely of his time and knowledge, and forwarded information in a number of letters. A list of Babcock marriages in Essex was published in *The Slade-Babcock Genealogical Newsletter.*

"William S. Appleton suggested that James Badcock was probably a cousin of George and Robert Badcock, early of Milton, Massachusetts Bay (then part of Dorchester, Mass.). Belle Preston mentioned a David Babcock as a member of the church in Dorchester in 1640, and said he was probably the father of George, who died in 1671, and Robert of Milton, and possibly of James, who was born in 1612, and Margaret, who died in 1705, aged 75. Margaret married in England a Henry Leland.

"In 1865 Appleton searched the Wivenhoe parish records and wrote that they contained no Badcocks at all [*NEHGR*, 19: 215]. Benton's article on Wivenhoe records did not contain a Badcock, nor did a

Badcock sign a 1619 petition of the principal inhabitants [Rickwood]. However, Appleton suggested there might have been Badcocks at Wivenhoe Cross, and that there were many in Essex, particularly at Great Bentley. Manors of Badcocks are located in Essex in the parish of Abberton (Adburton), eastwards of Layer de la Haye, a quarter mile northwest of the church, and at the village of East Thorp [Wright's *Essex*, 1:390; note remarks above by Mr. Noble]. The manor at Adburton passed out of the hands of the family before 1281 [Wright, 2:732].

"More work must be done if the English roots of the early New England Badcocks and Babcocks are to be traced with any certainty. Further, it should be stated that no Babcocks came to New England on the ship *Anne* in 1623. No Babcocks were listed in the Plymouth division of lands in 1624; in fact, none are found in the records of the colony until 1685. Nonetheless, the town records of Dartmouth, 20 June 1684 (1664 in Allen family sources...), George Badcock and Henry Tucker were mentioned as building a mill there [A. Borden, 26]."

One tradition which had persisted in the same Babcock family for generations, and which was not directly refuted in the preceding paragraph, was that the first Babcock had come over on the *Mayflower*. It is incredible how many had repeated this speculation as fact without even checking the *Mayflower* "passenger list," which is in print in a variety of books and journals, including *Ship Passenger Lists: National and New England (1600-1825)*, which contains a copy of William Bradford's "names of those which came over first, in ye year 1620" on pages 134-136. Months were spent tracing this rumor until finally this researcher received a photocopy of a typed copy of remarks made at a Babcock family reunion about a century ago, which included the comment that the Babcocks had been in America so long that for all the speaker knew they might have come on board the *Mayflower*. That piece of speculation was soon accepted as the truth.

Accuracy, the careful statement of proven fact, is dreadfully important. Yet, you must also be a little diplomatic. It is remarkable how many skeletons can be brought out of the family closet, even if equally remarkable is the experience of thousands that horse thieves are very difficult to find among your ancestors. Certainly you should repeat the stories of witchcraft and adultery recorded in colonial times, but a little care might be taken about revealing more recent events. Many genealogists have subscribed to an oath not to reveal data about illegitimate births during the past one hundred years. Living subjects may choose not to give a precise marriage date if they were married shortly before the birth of their first child. There is no harm in simply giving the year of marriage, or leaving the date out altogether. While it may be omitted, it should never be changed to conform to wishful thinking. The ancient records, however, should be copied in full; people have always had problems and it will not hurt the present generations to know that their own problems are nothing new.

Hopefully by this time the reader has understood a major point which might be repeated. The very reason why the decision to publish should be made at the earliest possible opportunity is that once you plan to go into print you will be more careful about research. Notes will contain bibliographical references, and quotations will be copied word for word with complete accuracy in transcribing precisely what was written, complete with every misspelling. Quotation marks must be used as they were intended, and any changes enclosed in brackets, those squared parentheses which look like []. A handbook of English will be very useful to many. A good thesaurus will aid some. The dictionary should be used by all.

The importance of consideration of structure and scope has been treated. It has been pointed out that family members are more likely to contribute needed data if the book to be produced will be of interest to all of them. The idea of the family being the primary customers once a book has been placed on sale has been discussed; all one needs for a financially successful genealogical publication is a list of one hundred interested adult relatives willing to share in the cost of manufacturing the final product, the family history book.

However, the problem of lost records requires further treatment. An illustration might help to prove this point. While this compiler was working on the Slade-Babcock project he did some research into his own Boyer and Dodge lines; this helped to fill the time while other data was being proven. In 1965 a letter was sent to cousin Townsend, with whom contact had been lost. His widow replied that he had died in 1963 and that all of his books, records and papers on the family had disappeared. The genealogist who does not publish should be aware that future generations will include without doubt a weak link, the person who is willing to throw things out without checking to see what is being discarded. Townsend's widow was not, most likely, the guilty party. When someone passes away there are many members of the family who are willing to "help clean up" and put reminders of the departed spouse out of sight of the grieving widow or widower. It may be months, or even years, before anyone realizes that the family heritage has gone into the trash.

It is true that most genealogies, and this book, are printed on cheaper papers which contain acid and will disintegrate in the years to come. However, it is a simple matter to provide a copy to the Genealogical

Society, 35 North West Temple, Salt Lake City, Utah 84150, with written permission to microfilm it. Such copies on film are then preserved in vaults deep in nearby mountains. In the meantime, your family history will be read by several generations to come and may well inspire others to revise, enlarge, update and republish the work.

Hopefully, now the reader is fully aware that publishing a family history is a big job. As succeeding chapters will show, however, there need be no expenses beyond those of many other hobbies, and the ultimate expense of manufacturing the book can be underwritten completely by prepaid orders from members of the family.

There remains the need to mention in this chapter that the family history may involve many different surnames. For each immigrant ancestor, or most remote ancestor known, there should be a separate section. The sections should be arranged alphabetically by the surname common to that family, even if the immigrant did not bear that name, and within that section the descendants of that immigrant in the direct line should be treated. Organization is fully treated in the fourth chapter. The same chapter will touch upon the need for explanatory introductory material, and for a bibliography and index.

Now that the decision to publish has been made, you must consider the establishment of a deadline. Members of a family must know that an effort is being made to complete a project within a limited time, particularly when they are being asked for their own genealogical and biographical data. Further, if one does not establish a deadline for publication it becomes all too easy to simply work on and on, thinking the job will be completed someday. In such circumstances the work is rarely ever finished.

RESEARCHING ANCESTORS

There are a number of good books on genealogical method. It is advisable to read several of them, for none contain advice on every aspect of research. Furthermore, the reading of several different titles will reinforce your learning, as similar ideas are presented in different ways. This chapter is not intended as a lesson on method, but rather as a general overview of some of the problems of this aspect of research. It will be most useful to beginners, but may be of some value to all.

Naturally one who has decided to "do the family history" will undertake this task, at least initially, with a great deal of enthusiasm. Each new discovery will be exciting, and sometimes the initial success may seem very great indeed. It is tempting to push ahead without stopping to consider that genealogical method is different from that of many other fields, and that the study of method should be a prerequisite to the continued search for one's ancestors.

Work in genealogy is so complex that efficiency and effectiveness must be matters of immediate concern. You can easily spend days searching aimlessly in libraries, or you can be well organized, doing everything in reasonable steps according to a well designed plan or system.

Building a personal genealogical library is of the utmost importance. As most books intended for use by genealogists are printed in rather small editions they tend to be rather expensive, perhaps running $18 to $40 per copy in 1991. Periodicals are generally limited in circulation to a few hundred or a few thousand subscribers. Most publishers of catalogs must charge for them, too. However, an intelligent selection of the literature will prevent the cost of a personal library from becoming prohibitive.

Gilbert H. Doane's *Searching for Your Ancestors*, a fine work on method first published in 1937 and revised in 1980 by James B. Bell, must now be ordered from the University of Minnesota Press at $15.95. While it was easier to obtain when it was published by Bantam Books, many communities have full service book stores willing to special order.

Doane's work will impress the reader with the fact that genealogical research can be done, but the most recent edition of *Genealogical & Local History Books in Print*, which would make an excellent second purchase, shows how much material is readily available! Netti Schreiner-Yantis, the compiler, will provide information to those who write to her at 6818 Lois Drive, Springfield, Virginia 22150. This resource lists not only books on method, with the addresses of vendors, but periodicals, source materials and family histories, with almost five thousand of them indexed by surname contents in the fourth edition, a 2143 page work which has proved to be not only of tremendous value as a guide to published materials but also as a marketing tool for the publisher.

A subscription to *The Genealogical Helper* is a must for beginners in the field. Information on this periodical and a catalog of other materials available from The Everton Publishers, Inc., may be obtained by making a request by postcard to this firm at P. O. Box 368, Logan, UT 84321, being sure to include one's name and address. This massive magazine, which is thoroughly indexed each issue, appears six times per year and contains about two hundred pages, eight and one-half by eleven inches, per copy. Within a year's subscription one will find lists of family organizations, societies, libraries and professional genealogists. Each issue contains some articles on method, often treating a particular region, and a huge quantity of ads, which are ever changing. Advertising in *The Genealogical Helper* has generally proven to be cost effective, but it is most helpful if the advertiser will maintain the same address over a period of years, for subscribers and readers often save ads for a long period before responding to them. This publisher has obtained excellent results from advertising books for sale. The rates are justified by the large circulation.

Another postcard to the Genealogical Publishing Company, Inc., 1001 North Calvert Street, Baltimore, Maryland 21202, requesting their most recent catalogs, will result in receipt of some of the few free catalogs available in this field. The first book ordered from this firm might well be *Genealogy as Pastime and Profession* by Donald Lines Jacobus, which should be read and reread several times over the course of the years. It is a mere 120 pages long and is priced moderately.

The first edition of this present work also recommended purchase from Genealogical Publishing of Jacobus' *Index to Genealogical Periodicals*, while stating that that work was "somewhat difficult to use because one has to consult several sections of it while seeking a family name, but no more useful work has ever been offered so compactly and reasonably in price, considering its scope." After considering the shortcomings of the original three volume edition this writer decided to produce an improved edition. This six family name indices were combined into one, with the same treatment accorded to the place and topic indices. Copies of this work are available from this writer, whose address is listed on the copyright page.

However, this is not the only index volume which should be purchased. Those who live at some distance from libraries will find that a comprehensive personal collection of index works, bibliographies and catalogs will allow time to plan the most effective research. As an aside, this compiler does travel to the Research Library at UCLA frequently, having planned his work in advance, but also photocopies materials rather than taking notes from them. Notes can then be taken at one's leisure, and the sources remain readily available in one's own files for checking at the proofreading stage.

This compiler's interests dictate that he keep current a collection of catalogs from Goodspeed's Book Shop, Inc., 7 Beacon Street, Boston, Massachusetts 02108, from Tuttle Antiquarian Books, Inc., P. O. Box 541, Rutland, Vermont 05701, and from Phillimore & Co. Ltd., Shopwyke Hall, Chichester, Sussex, England PO20 6BQ. In each case a postcard indicating one's interest in genealogy and local history catalogs with one's name and address will gain the current ordering information. These catalogs can be very useful as bibliographies. Heritage Books, Inc., 1540-E Pointer Ridge Place, Bowie, Maryland 20716-1859, and Southern Historical Press, Inc., P. O. Box 738, Easley, South Carolina 29641-0738, are among others offering worthwhile lists on a regular basis.

Other genealogical bookstores advertise in the *Helper* and *The Yellow Pages*. Most will have the seventh edition of *The Handy Book for Genealogists* in stock. The hardcover is a must, for a paper copy would soon be worn out. Within its 392 large pages this resource contains valuable material concerning the location of original records, manuscript collections and checklists of printed sources, as well as the names and addresses of principal libraries, archives and genealogical societies. The state maps, which show county boundaries, are most helpful. It should be remembered that without the patronage of area researchers, local genealogical bookstores, which provide a valuable service, would have to close their doors.

Also available from Genealogical Publishing is the new edition of *Genealogical Research: Methods and Sources*, edited by Milton Rubincam. It covers genealogy subject by subject, state by state and country by country. The same firm has produced Val D. Greenwood's *The Researcher's Guide to American Genealogy*, a very popular and helpful reference. Both of these titles are candidates for one's personal library. However, the most complete reference is *The Source: a Guidebook of American Genealogy*, edited by Arlene Eakle and Johni Cerny, and published by Ancestry Publishing Company, 350 South 400 East, Salt Lake City, Utah 84111. This immense work by sixteen genealogists contains 786 quarto pages, a magnificent effort updated with each printing and containing far more material than Greenwood's excellent book.

Three editions of P. William Filby's *American & British Genealogy & Heraldry*, a very helpful bibliography with many annotations, have been published, the latest by The New England Historic Genealogical Society, 101 Newbury Street, Boston, Mass. 02116. The index is particularly worthwhile. Filby has also done immensely valuable work on the bibliography and indexing of immigration and passenger lists, published in part by Gale Research, Inc., 236 Penobscot Building, Detroit, Michigan 48226-9948.

Ruth Wilder Sherman and Dr. David L. Greene have succeeded as editors of one of this compiler's favorite quarterly journals, *The American Genealogist*, founded by Donald Lines Jacobus. While intended to be national in scope, the majority of the articles submitted for publication are oriented towards the Northeast. For the researcher in other areas it still makes very good reading, as it is instructive in the area of scholarship. The book reviews are must reading for a person with a work in preparation. A one year subscription is $20. Send your check to The American Genealogist, 128 Massasoit Drive, Warwick, Rhode Island 02888-6307.

Genealogical Periodical Annual Index, a title available in many libraries, can be ordered from Heritage Books. It indexes the literature year by year and lists addresses from which copies of cited articles can be obtained. Two much older index works continue to prove their value over the years. Munsell's *The American Genealogist, Being a Catalogue of Family Histories* is a reprint of the fifth edition of 1900. Few Southern families are represented. More helpful is Munsell's *Index to American Genealogies; and to Genealogical Material Contained in All Works such as Town Histories, County Histories, Local Histories, Historical Society Publications, Biographies, Historical Periodicals, and Kindred Works*, also dating from 1900. Some will wish to postpone purchases of these earlier works until they have surveyed the more recent literature in genealogical bibliography.

These titles represent the nucleus of a personal library. They will provide a great deal of information allowing the reader to spend wisely when adding to his collection.

An index too large to be acquired for most personal collections is the forty-eight volume *American Genealogical Index* edited by Fremont Rider and published by the Godfrey Memorial Library of Middletown, Connecticut, between 1942 and 1952. This index is now being replaced by the even more comprehensive *American Genealogical-Biographical Index*, which has been appearing since 1952 at the rate of a few volumes a year, and is in the collections of numerous genealogical and research libraries. While its scope is limited, it is a very detailed index to hundreds of sources, some of which have been indexed nowhere else.

Reference librarians are invaluable consultants on the use of the various Union Lists of books, periodicals and manuscripts. The researcher working in secondary sources will want to know where many titles can be located, particularly as many older genealogies were printed in editions of less than 200 copies, and are not in the Library of Congress collection.

The biggest problem faced by the beginner is, however, that of geneagraphy, the evaluation of these works. Assiduous reading of book reviews in *The American Genealogist* and the *National Genealogical Society Quarterly* will remind the researcher that many works in print are truly poor. Virtually all contain errors, if only due to the tremendous mass of data contained in them. Over the years one learns to evaluate secondary sources. Were they written well? Did they list sources? Were a bibliography and index provided? Were impossible claims made? One genealogy even goes so far as to list three generations of ancestry for Adam! No western line can be documented generation by generation further back than about 500 A.D.

It becomes clear, then, that the value of printed works pales next to that of the original records. Millions of documents are available in thousands of record offices, whether they be birth, marriage and death certificates, marriage license applications, census returns, wills, deeds, or court, church, military and cemetery records. Yet even the primary records are not infallible, and the work of Noel C. Stevenson on the evaluation of evidence can prove most helpful in this regard.

It has been mentioned that this chapter is not meant as a "how to" piece. Rather it must be primarily a caveat, a warning that there are many pitfalls. Those seeking organized help will find that many genealogical societies and community colleges offer courses (though generally not for college credit) in genealogical methods. In some towns these courses are also offered to small groups privately, in people's homes, at low cost. It can be very helpful to take such a course. Not only will knowledge of the approach to research, correspondence and evaluation be enhanced, but conversation among the students will also highlight successful ways of solving particular problems.

Correspondence courses in genealogy are also available. The Home Study Department of Brigham Young University, Provo, Utah, will send a catalog on request. BYU's college courses are for credit, and are transferable. The titles vary from time to time. Non-Mormons are allowed to omit those lessons concerning LDS beliefs and concentrate on methods of research. BYU's costs are very reasonable.

The National Genealogical Society, 4527 Seventeenth Street, North, Arlington, Virginia 22207 (telephone [703] 525-0050), offers a correspondence course as well. In addition, the NGS circulates books to members by mail (as do a number of other societies) and publishes its *Quarterly*, national in scope, with excellent book reviews.

A systems approach to publishing a family history will soon prove helpful. Every step in the process can take a great deal of time. Waiting for data can take months, and involved repeated prodding. If results are poor it may be wise to reread Greenwood's chapter on "Successful Correspondence," or buy an entire book on the subject.

However, returning to the idea of a system, you must begin to think in terms not only of researching ancestors but of locating all possible living relatives, at least all of the second, third and fourth cousins who can be found. Once this book has been read through it will be obvious there are many other things to be done at the same time, such as looking at typewriters or computers intended for the production of the final camera-ready copy. Is it time to advertise? What should the page size be? How do you build a mailing list? What about copyright and listing in *Books in Print*? What reviewers might be interested in the work? You must think not just of researching ancestors, but about the whole system of publishing as well. A systems approach will allow you to maximize your achievements with minimal waste.

Nonetheless, having done research in secondary sources (assuming you knew enough about your family to do so), and having recognized that many of them are of value only as sources of clues, it is time to put your efforts into the primary records. A few observations concerning the various types of records are in order, even if this work leaves detailed explanations to Doane, Greenwood, Eakle and Cerny, Rubincam, Williams and others. You must always consider the origins, immediacy and authority of primary sources.

Vital records, those of births, marriages and deaths, and baptismal and burial records as well, can be invaluable. However, in some cultures one's family is traced strictly through the maternal side, the assumption being that motherhood is the only certain factor! Depending on the locality involved, it may be easy to work back in a number of lines through published or original vital records, or it may be virtually impossible.

Typically, a birth record will name both parents, perhaps giving their ages at the time of the birth of the child, and probably their places of birth, as well as other details to varying degrees. The marriage record of the parents may then prove to be readily accessible in the same place as the birth of the child. Sometimes it may be necessary to turn to the probate indexes, however, to determine when the parents died, if their estates went through probate at all. The probate files will frequently reveal helpful information. While death certificates were less readily filed in early years and birth and marriage records, they often contain data concerning place and date of birth, and parentage. In difficult cases the probate records may record the place of burial, leading you to tomb-stones, cemetery or mortuary records. Newspaper obituaries can also be located, and often contain family history. Thus you can go back a generation and start the process over again with birth records.

If using vital records worked consistently, tracing a line would be simple, but of course there are huge gaps in extant records, and often no record was made at all, if only because the parents could not afford the fee involved in having the birth recorded in the town or county books, or objected to paying the Stamp Tax. Indeed the longest and most carefully proven pedigree based on vital records would be very dull, totally lacking in biographical detail or historical background.

If you are fortunate you will trace your family back far enough to allow the use of county histories, topographies and other secondary sources as clues. This simplifies searching in original records, but does not preclude the possibility that the secondary sources were compiled by individuals who used original sources, or tradition, carelessly. This compiler began to recheck the work in books not so much because he was interested in the technical process of establishing evidence beyond reasonable doubt, but because he believed that completing the records for each of the children of an ancestral couple, insofar as births, marriages and deaths were concerned, would translate into higher sales.

Routine checking of vital records will demonstrate that the original entries do contain errors, and in some cases outright falsehoods. Further-more, some records are more complete than others. The birth certificate of one child might contain considerably more data on the parents than that of a sibling, whose certificate was completed by a less careful doctor or clerk, perhaps dependant upon information given by an overly tired mother or a father with other things on his mind.

As for fabrications, Ella Harriet Talbot consistently lied about her age, so that by the time she died people believed she was much younger than she really was. The information on death certificates comes from survivors or sometimes friends who may not be certain of the details. The correct age of Ella Talbot was finally determined through tracking her, decade by decade, in the census. Hopefully the 1850 census, which listed her as aged four, was accurate. In any event, a lady whose year of birth was given as 1862 on her death certificate was born in late 1845!

When official vital records are lacking, other kinds of evidence can often be used to solve problems. Many family Bibles have been passed down and are preserved today, sometimes centuries after they were first purchased. While these Bibles may be very difficult to locate, the researcher who does trace living relatives may be rewarded with the news that one of them has these important Bible records. It is still necessary to evaluate the entries, however, to see if they were likely entered as the events occurred. A good methods manual deals with this problem in detail.

Nonetheless, records in family Bibles are often more accurate and easily accessible than church records. Many ministers and priests were inattentive to the task of keeping their records in order. Frequently entries were made months after the fact from slips of paper which often contained incomplete notations, and which were occasionally mixed out of order. Some records were kept by the parish, while others were kept by ministers who took their books with them from one church to another. The record of the marriage of Samuel Dodge Boyer and Judith Debozear, which took place in Philadelphia in 1855, came from an affidavit by the minister made years later when he was residing in Indiana, stating that he had recorded it in his book. Had not Judith Debozear Boyer applied for a widow's pension following the loss of her husband in the Civil War, the record would have been lost to her descendants.

Newspapers can be particularly helpful, for once a probate file, death certificate, tombstone or even an unreliable secondary source has provided a place and date of death, an obituary can frequently be located. A growing number of works containing genealogical abstracts from newspapers is being published in article and book form, and numerous newspapers are available on microforms in college and university libraries. In addition, consultation with the reference librarians at these schools will frequently help to find other materials, including special obituary indexes.

While it may often be necessary for a researcher to hire someone to locate and copy a specific obituary, the place and date of death will often suggest a specific paper, in the early days a weekly with a limited number of pages, so that the search can be made quickly at a reasonable cost. There are a number of guides listing newspapers, their dates of publication, and the location of collections. These volumes can be found in many city, genealogical and college libraries, and are usually described in research manuals. The staff of your local newspaper will frequently help, allowing you to search quickly through their copy of the current newspaper guide, which, however, will not list those papers no longer being published.

County histories, mug books and most nineteenth-century genealogies, as well as many of those published recently, are of limited value because they abound with errors. In most cases the compilers, well meaning but untrained in scientific methods of research, simply assembled data from a great variety of sources. However, if the clues contained therein are followed, much time can often be saved.

Do not overlook checking all possible genealogies. For example, the identity of Deborah, wife of Job Babcock of Westerly and South Kingston, Rhode Island, was not revealed in Stephen Babcock's book on the family, nor was it found in the vital records. However, Job and Deborah Babcock had children known to have married into the Hull, Segar, Reynolds and Hoxie families, and a check of the Hoxie genealogy showed that Deborah was a Reynolds, as proven by the inventory of her father's estate. It does help to peruse available genealogies concerning all the spouses of all the children of a particular couple under study.

Some knowledge of library science can be very helpful in obtaining the secondary sources needed. Those who have had no training in research in any field at the university level will find it most desirable to establish rapport with a local librarian who has had the necessary training. This person can explain, among other things, interlibrary loan services, which may vary from town to town and state to state, but which are usually offered at reasonable cost.

Union Lists are an invaluable tool. These catalogs, usually in bound form, reveal where a particular book or periodical can be located. State libraries may have fair to excellent collections which circulate on an interlibrary loan basis. Other libraries provide photocopying services. However, these services can vary greatly in price and quality of service. For example, an order to the New York Public Library may elicit the response that payment must be made in full before the order can be processed, and this may include an order fee of several dollars, a fee for each page to be copied, a mailing fee, and even a cost of living surcharge! A similar request to the New York State Library has been answered with the requested material being sent by return mail with a bill for copying services of a few cents per page only. Thus be advised to sample the services of several different libraries if much photoduplication is to be requested. It would seem that the Library of Congress and the New York Public Library are much slower to respond than many other libraries with large holdings. Historical societies can be very helpful, as can some state agencies where the staff is truly dedicated to their work. In all cases, orders should be clear and concise, and accompanied by a self-addressed stamped envelope. Pay fees promptly if billed, and send a word of thanks to anyone providing really good service.

It would be wise to advertize interests not only in *The Genealogical Helper* but in publications of the societies which offer a limited number of free queries to members. All queries should be specific, including names, a place and a date, or a precise statement of the problem. Most genealogists will not waste their time corresponding with anyone who asks for all data on the Smith, Jones and Johnson families. Even a query requesting information on the parentage of John Brown of Rehoboth, Massachusetts, will be ignored by those most likely able to help. After all, there were many John Browns in Rehoboth over the years, several at any given time. A query asking about John and Lydia Brown of Rehoboth, living there in 1780, might be answered with a question as to which one of the three couples answering this description is the one under study.

Correspondence resulting from queries should be answered with thanks and a stamp representing token payment. Good manners may well trigger the donor of data to keep one's problem in mind, or mention it to someone else who might be of assistance. On the other hand, queries will result in requests for information which the compiler does not have. A specific query asking for the parentage of John Brown who married Lydia Bullock in Rehoboth in 1762 has generated requests for information on all of the Brown families of Missouri in 1870! When this compiler receives such letters he replies politely but negatively if an SASE (self addressed stamped envelope) is enclosed, and not at all otherwise.

All correspondence of value should be filed in an orderly fashion. The filing system is discussed in many manuals and some specialized handbooks. Unfortunately, the need for the system does not become obvious in the early stages of research. However, it pays to give filing attention from the beginning if a tremendous amount of work is to be avoided later, usually at the very moment you are desperate to avoid such housekeeping chores. A filing cabinet, preferably a steel one which can stand constant use, a large supply of manila folders, and a Rolodex should be purchased. Surname and place folders should be labeled, as well as folders which will contain letters from correspondents who discuss a number of surnames in one letter. The folders should contain a catalog sheet, and calendar of documents or cross-reference calendar as may be necessary. For example, a letter from Jonathan James dealing primarily with the Sherman family but mentioning an Evans problem in passing could be placed either in an HIJ folder in the correspondence section of the filing system, or in the Sherman file. In any case there should be notations made in other files (including Evans) that such a letter can be found in a certain folder, and Jonathan James' address, and perhaps telephone number, should be kept in the Rolodex. Rolodex cards should be dated as a reminder of how many years have elapsed since ideas were exchanged. This failure to date material has led to the collapse of more than one surname service which failed to query participants regularly to check if they had moved.

This latter point brings to the surface the problem of a compiler having a consistent address. It is a nightmare for correspondents when someone moves a few blocks without leaving a forwarding address, or when the forwarding address has expired. All too often an envelope full of information for a correspondent is returned to await the chance that his name might be spotted in a journal with a new address. Letterheads would be of greater value if they contained both a current address and a more permanent one, perhaps that of a close relative. As for being a publisher, the only thing you need is a stable address.

Once the preliminary research has been finished it is time to write, edit and create a final draft for circulation to those relatives and genealogists who have demonstrated valuable knowledge of the lines involved. The details of the format of the draft are discussed in the fourth chapter below. There are implications concerning copyright in the circulation of drafts. Generally, draft copies containing the name of the author, the copyright symbol and the date are protected legally, if not practically, from infringement. This compiler usually stamps his drafts with his name and address and the date. However, this is done not for copyright purposes but merely to identify the origin and the time it was made, the time being important to anyone who might see more than one draft and want to know the chronology of changes in the text. Of course drafts may contain materials not to be found in the published book, and chronology is an important tool of evaluation. Later drafts, therefore, are often considered more reliable, all else being equal. Many genealogists do not look upon the copyright as protection, feeling that it is useful not only as a marketing tool in a field where unauthorized reprinting cannot be rewarded by profits as a particular family history has limited appeal. Nonetheless, the copyright of a draft no longer expires in twenty-eight years, but now lasts the lifetime of the author plus fifty years.

The circulation of drafts is most important in those projects in which a family newsletter has not been used as an interim method of allowing for critical response. The reviewers were kind when *Slade-Babcock Genealogy* appeared, any many were apparently impressed with the "fine young genealogist" who published it. To laudatory comments, however, must come the reply that publishing a good genealogy can be easy if you are willing to make the effort to pick other people's brains.

As the drafts begin to take on final form it is wise to notify appropriate societies and journals of the working title and the scope of work in progress. This will generate increased correspondence and criticism in response to wider circulation of drafts, as well as more names for the list of potential customers.

Many errors will be corrected in the draft stage, and as corrections are offered the drafts can be retyped (or edited on the computer) and recirculated as needed. Those intended as final drafts must be most carefully proofread for spelling, syntax and punctuation as they are completed in precisely the same format as the camera-ready copy is intended to have. A quick check of the number of spaces used in a line of the final draft against the number used on the camera-ready copy is one way to spot typographical errors often overlooked in proofreading.

Proofreading requires tremendous attentiveness and presents a great problem. In work in family history it is important to read not only for grammar and spelling, sentence structure, proper tense, verb agreement and antecedents as one might proof a novel, but to check against original materials to see that the factual data have been copied properly through the many drafts. A final check for logical chronology and location may be made at this point, too. Of course chronology may seem illogical if the compiler does not understand the variety of dating systems used in different colonies before 1752, as mentioned above. One good technique of proofreading is to start reading sentences in reverse order to determine how well each one stands on its own.

Computer spell checking should also be used once the copy has been read several times. It will reveal some strange errors!

Once the "final" drafts concerning the ancestral lines have been finished, circulated and double-checked, you will want to concentrate on filling out the records of your living relatives. It will be wise, while that is being done, to continue to read the journals, if only checking the tables of contents and the book reviews for materials which might be helpful. For the very reason that new articles of value, new ideas for research, or criticism of interest may be published in the interim, it is wise to postpone the processing of the camera-ready copy until the entire book has been put into "final draft" form. After the camera-ready copy and indexing is finished it may still seem wise to add appendices.

RESEARCHING LIVING RELATIVES

The importance of the search for, and inclusion of, living relatives in your family history has been stressed. The purpose, again, is twofold. First, your living relatives will be the primary customers for the published genealogy. Second, some of them, at least, are most likely to be valuable sources of information who will contribute freely if they know that their knowledge will be published.

The scope of the search will be decided in part by the makeup of the family under study. The greater the difficulty in tracing the ancestral lines, the greater the effort should be to locate living relatives. This compiler has had the good fortune to be able to discover over two hundred families in his and his wife's ancestry, and during the search to enter into correspondence with dozens of genealogists interested in purchasing his work, once it was published. Many others will have similar good fortune, and it will become apparent that including every single living relative, many of whom will be related no more closely than eighth cousin, would make the final size of the text unmanageable.

There are many genealogies in print which run to a length of six hundred pages or more and include only the descendants of one immigrant couple. Thus you cannot contemplate compiling a work including all the descendants of over two hundred immigrant ancestors! Indeed, some of these family histories have been published by large committees or family associations, some of which worked over a period of many years, handing down their files from one generation to the next.

However, if you are a fourth generation American, and can trace none of the immigrant ancestors to their origins in England, Germany, Armenia, Argentina or China, as the case may be, all living relatives must be traced as far as possible, and it may prove desirable to expand the scope to include as many data as possible about the ancestry of the spouses of the blood relatives. Most of these spouses can provide their parentage and data on their grandparents without great difficulty, and will be glad to be included to such an extent.

In any event, if the origins of the family have already been lost, no more time can be wasted writing down what scraps of information remain. Blacks, American Indians, descendants of Chinese immigrants and others about whom there may be little documentation in early generations will find much oral history which should be recorded on tape without delay. The richness of this sort of family history has been demonstrated in a number of articles in the *Washington Post* and the *Los Angeles Times*. Where hard data may be in short supply, the biographical details passed down by families make fascinating social history.

No doubt there are many who have few siblings and only a small number of first cousins. Indeed, this writer has only two sisters, one first cousin on his father's side, and four first cousins on his mother's side. The number of second cousins, however, is larger, simply because families tended to be greater in size in the late nineteenth century than they were in the early twentieth century. Third and fourth cousins are numerous, and scattered all over the United States and England, to say nothing of those who have lived at least temporarily in other countries.

Let us consider the case of a family living today, in which, for the sake of illustration, the genealogist is forty years old, and married with three children. This person also has two siblings, each of them married with three children. Most of these nine children were born almost twenty years ago, and among the three siblings of the generation approaching middle age there may be some grandchildren, perhaps two or three. This does not make a very large family group.

However, the group becomes larger if the parents of the genealogist and his or her spouse were in each case one of four children, and there were five children in the preceding generation, with perhaps seven in the one before that. Furthermore, perhaps the origins and parentage of the immigrant ancestors are unknown, but descendants of their siblings can be located.

If all the ancestors of the family historian had come to the country about 1855, and thus genealogist was of the fourth or fifth generation, a large number of people would be involved in his work. First of all, a person in the fourth generation would have eight immigrant ancestors, and if the spouse had a similar family there would be eight more subject to study on that side. These sixteen immigrants, making eight couples, might have had, between them, about fifty children, of whom perhaps forty married and had families of their own, averaging four children, so that the eight couples in the first generation would have one hundred and sixty grandchildren. If one hundred and twenty of these married and had an average of three children, that would make three hundred sixty members of the fourth generation! If only one hundred of the latter generation are interested sufficiently in the family history to purchase a copy of the finished work, there will be at least enough to pay all the costs of book manufacturing. Additional copies should be printed, of course, and the question of how many will be dealt with in the fifth chapter, below.

As mentioned previously, circumstances led this compiler to do his first book on the ancestors and descendants of one couple, who were both born shortly after 1800. Their ancestry was traced to families with fifty-four different surnames. Benjamin Slade was of the sixth generation of his family, and his wife, Angeline Babcock, was of the seventh in hers. They had twelve children, of whom eight grew to maturity, married and had one or more children of their own. Benjamin and Angeline had thirty grandchildren, born from 1856 to 1890. Of these only twelve married and had children who lived long enough to survive their parents. Of these twelve in the eighth generation of the Slade family, four had one child each, four had families limited to two children, two had four children, one had six, and one had nine. Thus there were thirty-five in the ninth generation, but only twenty-four married and had their own families.

Of the twenty-four in the ninth generation who had their own families, twenty-one were living in 1964 and of these eighteen were living at the time the book appeared in March of 1971. These people had been born from 1886 to 1918. Four of them had one child, fourteen had two children, two had three, two had four, one had five, and one had seven children. Thus fifty-eight were born into the tenth generation, and of these forty-two were recorded as having families by 1970. The tenth generation having been born from 1907 to 1954, the youngest was only sixteen in 1970, and there were several marriages imminent.

There were forty in the tenth generation who had families by 1970. Eight had had one child, sixteen had had two, nine had three, four had four, and three had five children each. So there were ninety-eight children recorded by the compiler in the eleventh generation by 1970. Four were living but not recorded until later, and a number were born after 1970. Twenty-three children of the next generation were of record that year, the oldest born in 1958.

Nine members of the ninth generation purchased the book. Eighteen members of the tenth did so, and three of the eleventh. However, some of the family bought a number of copies; ninety were sold on a prepublication basis, mostly to the family and some corresponding genealogists. One was sold to a neighbor down the street who was curious as to how a family history would look. In short, the sales were sufficient to cover the cost of printing and binding, with $20 left over, in spite of the fact that this publisher had no knowledge whatsoever of book marketing techniques at that time.

Ideally, prepublication sales will result in receipts large enough to pay for the cost of book manufacturing, the scope of the work having been broad enough to attract the necessary number of customers but narrow enough to have allowed the size of the project to be manageable. As this compiler knew nothing of marketing he based his first printing order on the ninety prepublication orders and requested that only two hundred copies of *Slade-Babcock Genealogy* be produced. The shipment included twenty "overs." A miniscule marketing effort limited to having the book copyrighted, the placing of a few small ads in *The Genealogical Helper*, distribution of three or four copies to reviewers, and the mailing of perhaps 500 flyers over a period of years, as well as word of mouth, resulted in the remainder being sold in about seven years. The additional sales paid the balance on the IBM Selectric used in making the camera-ready copy, all marketing, and, ultimately, several pieces of furniture.

Even though the profit could only have been measured in terms of a few pennies per hour invested, there was a great deal of satisfaction derived from having completed the first book. In addition, however, there was a sense of loss which had not been anticipated. The genealogy bug would not die, and three more projects were begun as soon as the reviews, which were most encouraging, appeared. These projects were published in one volume, *Ancestral Lines*, in 1975.

Having structured the work so that the size of the project will remain manageable, and there will be enough pre-publication customers to pay for manufacturing the volume, you should consider the input living relatives will have in addition to providing data on their own families, as well as the encouragement to complete the work. Scrapbooks, old certificates, genealogical notes and ancient photographs were unearthed by the descendants of Benjamin and Angeline (Babcock) Slade. Photocopies, transcripts and negative copies were provided to the compiler. Indeed, some relatives worked very hard to assist in collecting materials, and some were able to identify the subjects of family portraits made more than seventy-five years before.

While in the case of this work it was possible to locate all the living relatives within the scope of the projects, lost relatives can be found in a variety of ways, depending on the amount of documentation they left behind. Letters to the editor of weekly newspapers, or ads placed in these publications, may elicit help from friends of lost relatives in places to which members of the family have moved years before. Telephone books, motor vehicle records, probate files and deeds can be employed in tracing relatives. Ads in the "Bureau of Missing Ancestors" in *The Genealogical Helper* provide a fair return for the expense involved.

Both private and government agencies can help. The Salvation Army, the Veterans Administration and the Social Security Administration can help in some cases, under certain constraints. One organization which helps to establish contact between adopted children and their natural parents, in cases where all the parties seek contact, is ALMA, of 157 West Fifty-seventh Street, Room 504, New York, New York 10019.

The greatest assistance from relatives came in the area of circulating a form which this researcher devised, a "Family History Questionnaire."

This was printed sideways on eight and one-half by eleven inch paper and circulated to members of the family with covering form letters, each written specifically for circulation to a particular branch of the descendants of Benjamin Slade. Thus while the questionnaire was printed in a quantity of one thousand, the covering letters were addressed, for example, "To the Descendants of Walter Henry Salisbury," and were reproduced by Xerox.

The questionnaire, reproduced minus the heading on pages 48 and 49, had the title, "Family History Questionnaire," running across the top. The portion reproduced on page 46 was printed on the left side of the sheet, and the other was printed on the right. While the questionnaire is largely self-explanatory, the reasons for some of the questions raised might not be obvious.

Several genealogists have commented on this compiler's desire to collect the details of schooling, publications and the like. However, the wish was not so much that of a need to stress educational accomplishments, but to preserve the data which might lead to the uncovering of additional information from various sources. Information on religious preference can obviously lead to further study of church records. When an occupation is known all sorts of records may prove useful, such as those involved with licensing, union membership, trade associations, company newsletters, or group insurance. Military records may contain not only the details of service, but also of bonuses, land bounty warrants, and applications for retirement benefits or widows' pensions, all of which may reveal later places of residence and other data necessary to prove an entitlement.

The information on titles of publications was requested when it became apparent that this could lead to data in the Library of Congress and other sources of biography. Schools maintain cumulative records which often record the date and place of birth of a student, his parentage, and perhaps the names of his siblings. Alumni associations can often provide the last known address of a subject. Many colleges and universities have published histories of graduating classes, or at least directories of graduates. Some institutions may have been left bequests which might help you to find probate records or death certificates, which in turn may lead to living descendants. Thus the questionnaire requests information which was not only of immediate interest but also data which might lead to other avenues of research.

This particular form was typed on an IBM Executive typewriter, the model with variable spacing. This machine has various type widths, some two units wide, most of them three units wide, and some measuring four or five units across the face. Spacing between words can be two or three units, depending upon which space bar is hit with the thumb, or more, if more strokes on the space bars are made. As the type is larger than standard, there are fewer than six lines per inch, vertically. Thus it is possible to type copy with an Executive which can be reduced to the standard six lines per inch, allowing the questionnaire to be filled out on any standard typewriter, while at the same time reducing the length of the lines, so that a long one, such as "Full maiden name of spouse's mother," containing thirty-five characters and consuming almost three inches of elite type, and much more when typed on an IBM Executive, could be reduced to two and three-quarter inches, leaving a couple of inches for the name, and more if the margin is used, as it is invariably.

If the preceding is not very clear, it may be helpful to describe how the camera-ready copy of a questionnaire can be prepared on a standard typewriter, that is, any machine which in single space types precisely six lines per inch. The important point to keep in mind is that the final copy should be reduced so that "Full maiden name of spouse's mother" will not take up too much space.

Therefore, it would be wise to use a typewriter capable of being set at four lines per inch, leaving half a line of blank space between each two lines of type. If you do not have an extra wide carriage on your machine, as well as a stock of paper fourteen by seventeen inches in size (seventeen by twenty-two inch sheets available from many printers can be cut down), you will have to type the copy for the questionnaire on several sheets and paste them together, which is most likely since few typewriters come with a carriage at least seventeen inches wide.

White paper with a smooth surface and no watermark will do. Some may wish to use "repro" paper available from specialty stores dealing with printers and artists, but duplicator paper sold by the local stationery store will serve just as well. Duplicator paper is the type used on ditto machines, but many types of papers used for photocopying purposes have similar qualities.

Using a typewriter with a carbon ribbon is a necessity for any camera-ready work. Either a correcting ribbon or a product such as Liquid Paper or Snopake should be used in correcting errors. Only a carbon ribbon will produce copy of the quality necessary for the production of copies by lithography.

The samples printed in this book can be used as a guide to determine whether any changes should be made or not. If not, the only need is to type a new copy as a rough draft for sizing, leaving a half line of blank space between each two lines of type. The space from the top of the first line to the underlining at the bottom was originally printed as seven and one-quarter inches (and then slightly reduced for these pages). This included forty-three lines of typing and spacing. If these forty-three lines are typed with a half line of blank space between lines, there will be forty-two half-lines of blank space, totaling with the typed area sixty-four full lines of coverage, which, at six lines per inch, would occupy ten and two-thirds inches, necessitating the use of eight and one-half by thirteen (or fourteen) inch paper for typing the copy, since most typewriters do not handle typing close to the top and bottom margins well.

If the copy is being typed for reproduction at exactly two-thirds the size of the original, the length of each typed line will also shrink the same amount. If the width of the line when printed is to be about 4.8 inches, the line of the original copy should be 7.2 inches long. You should know whether you are using a machine with pica or elite type. Finding out which is simple. Type twelve x's in a row. If the line is one inch long the type face is elite, the smaller of the two. Twelve characters of pica type occupy one and one-fifth inches on a line. A line of seventy-two characters and spaces of pica type will equal 7.2 inches, and eighty-seven characters of elite type will equal 7.25 inches. Elite type allows more words per page, but may be less readable if reduced sharply. The copy for the third edition of this book was done in pica type one lines five and three-tenths in width, and then reduced to 88% of the original size. While a 10% reduction will not affect readability much, a 17% is about as far as one might dare to go with elite type. Twenty per cent might prove satisfactory with pica type for a book length work, and 25% has proven successful with some kinds of material.

For the questionnaire, however, a reduction to two-thirds of the original size should prove satisfactory. Some may not like having to use a magnifying glass to read it, however, and for those people one might make enlarged Xerox copies.

To proceed step by step, place an eight and one-half by fourteen sheet in your typewriter, leaving a margin of three-quarters of an inch on the left (with about one and one-half inches at the top). Allow for a typed line of 7.2 inches. If duplicating the form in this book, for which permission is granted, simply type, using a pica machine, on the first line, "Please fill in this form as completely as possible. Estimate dates [here hit return] where not definitely known, but always mark estimates with a question [return] mark or remarks explaining them." Do not include the quotation marks when typing, leave one space after the comma, and two spaces at the end of any sentence.

Then strike the return twice and type "Full name of subject" followed by the underline key until the full line is exactly 7.2 inches in length. As you continue typing it is important to remember that you can type a line several characters too short, but you must never type a line even one character too long. Many of us, when hyphenating a word at the end of a line, really need to consult a dictionary. This writer, with more than a dozen titles under his belt, still looks up words frequently to make sure hyphenation is correct. If your ignorance is not to be preserved for all time, you must use the dictionary frequently. Furthermore, little mistakes will reflect a disregard for detail which will not be well received by genealogists, particularly the reviewers.

Once you have typed the left side of the questionnaire the right side will come easily. The composer may wish to consider the question of whether the name and address of the researcher should be typed on the camera-ready copy. If your address is likely to change the area for the name and address can be left blank, to be rubber stamped later. In the makeup of the original, it was decided to leave the area blank for two reasons. First, copies of the form could be given to others who might want to have more printed for their own use (a printed address could still have been deleted using Liquid Paper), and second, some family members who circulate the form to their close relatives will want the sheets returned to them directly to they can look them over before forwarding them to the compiler.

With both sides typed there remains the task of pasting them together and providing a heading. Recommendations of printers notwithstanding, this publisher continues to encourage the use of rubber cement for this purpose. The two halves of the questionnaire can be pasted, making sure that once the cement has had time to dry all excess is wiped off. Then a heading, such as "Family History Questionnaire," can be pasted across the top. It is wise to mark a measured line on the paper with a nonreproducing pencil (light blue or light purple) before the pasting is done to allow the heading to be affixed perfectly straight. The eye is simply not as good as a ruler for this purpose.

Once you have done this there remains nothing but taking the copy to the printer and telling him the percentage to which the printed form should be reduced as well as the quantity needed.

The letters circulated to living relatives are very important. A single form letter to all relatives will prove to be much less effective than more specific form letters to smaller family groups. The letters should contain some explanation of the compiler's project, the relationship between the compiler and those to whom the letter is addressed, some directions for completion of the form, and mention of the book in preparation. An example follows:

CARL BOYER, 3rd
P. O. Box 333
Santa Clarita, CA 91322-0333

November 11, 1969

To the descendants of Walter Henry Salisbury:

As you may know, your ancestor Walter Henry Salisbury was descended from Benjamin and Angeline (Babcock) Slade, a couple who lived in New York State during the first three-quarters of the nineteenth century. For the past five years I have been working to trace the family history of Benjamin and Angeline back to the immigrant ancestors, who were among the earlier settlers of Massachusetts and the first settlers of Rhode Island.

Now I am completing a study of the descendants of Benjamin and Angeline so that the ancestors and descendants of this couple can be published in a book to be called *Slade-Babcock Genealogy*.

Jesse E. Salisbury, Philip H. Salisbury and Bessie M. Connett have already provided me with some information on your family, and to save you time I have entered this data on the enclosed Family History Questionnaire. I would truly appreciate your completing the form as much as possible and returning it to me in the enclosed stamped, self-addressed envelope. It is important to return the form as soon as possible so that the organizing and collecting of data can continue through the youngest generations to completion. Therefore, please do not plan to do any research before completing the form, but merely answer each question as well as you can. If you would write a short biography of both the subject and spouse on the reverse it would make the book more interesting. I do need to have the questionnaire returned by December 5th. However, additional information received a few weeks later can be included in the final draft.

It may interest you to know that while I am not directly related to you, my wife is a descendant of Slade Peter Vandenbergh, who was, like Walter Henry Salisbury, a grandson of Benjamin and Angeline. Compiling family history is my hobby, and I am personally bearing all the expenses of this research.

Once the book has been completed you will be advised when prepublication sales are taking place. The book will be offered to you, but please understand that there will be no obligation to buy a copy. I will be disappointed, however, if I cannot include every living descendant of Benjamin and Angeline in the *Slade-Babcock Genealogy*.

A copy of your entry in the book will be returned to you for possible corrections several weeks before the text will be sent to the printers.

I would like to thank you in advance for your help.

Sincerely,

[hand signed]

The results of such form letters have been good. Returns can be enhanced by adding handwritten notes to the letters as they are mailed out. Some, however, will not answer unless reminded individually, and politely, that 100% participation in needed to make the family history a worthwhile volume. If the historian will keep the original copy of each letter on file, additional Xerox copies can be sent with another questionnaire and SASE, with a notation in the margin such as, "I have heard from both of your brothers but not you or your sister. I would really appreciate hearing from you shortly so the book can be complete." These reminders must be mailed on the deadline date to make the maximum impression. Indeed, it is often wise to mail questionnaires to those who have responded asking for help with those who have not.

Occasionally a telephone call will help establish rapport with those who might not otherwise reply. Incomplete questionnaires should not be returned for completion until the data has been copied, lest the form be lost. People who receive a form partially completed in a familiar hand will be more likely to respond.

Once a book has been published, one more letter should be sent to those who did not reply, requesting data for the revised edition, or a planned supplement. It is remarkable how those who had not responded at all may buy the book as well as cooperate in providing the information missing from the first edition.

Indeed, it may be possible to elicit further information immediately prior to publication of the work if the material returned to each member of the family contains some comment, for those who did not respond, concerning the reason for the lack of data. This comment should be couched in neutral terms designed to avoid "putting down" those who did not cooperate.

The organization of the data gathering is designed to allow the older generations to provide some material on the younger members of the family, generation by generation. Thus several forms might be sent with one letter, asking for partial completion of all of them. Parents, for example, may be able to complete the data on their own children and grandchildren fairly well, leaving the children only to fill in the ancestry of the spouse and some other details. Remember that each spouse should have his or her own generation number from the immigrant ancestor of that surname, or none at all. This compiler did try to include the parents and grandparents of each spouse with the thought that such material, easily obtained at the present, might be more difficult to gather in the future. In those cases where any grandparent was foreign born, a greater effort was made to determine whether that person was the first generation to come to the United States, or whether parents or grandparents also migrated, so that this information might be included, lest it be forgotten later.

Many spouses were interested in the family history, in the fact that it could be done, and a few requested information on how they could compile their own, which is, in part, the reason for publication of this tome. Nevertheless, you must be careful to stay within the scope of the project as originally designed as much as possible.

The older relatives will have been contacted as soon as the work of compiling the descendants has begun, if not during the stage of compiling the ancestry, a point at which some might have contributed clippings, scrapbooks, manuscript genealogy and photographs. The latter, by the way, could be duplicated and sold as separate packets, suitable for framing, rather than included in the book.

The older relatives will fail to complete the forms as fully as might be expected, leaving gaps in the material being sought. As this point it may be necessary to interview these people personally or by telephone, on an individual basis. Personal interviews will allow more time for the compiler to think about how to phrase questions, but telephone interviews can be completed in stages, further calls being made as a review of the materials at hand suggests more questions. If a tape recorder is used it will still be necessary to take quick notes, for scanning them during the interview helps to keep the conversation coming back to the subject, even if some digressions will provide useful color for the biographical entries. It certainly helps if you are a quick thinker.

An interview might go something like this:

Question: "On your questionnaires you did not put down the year your father was born, or his date of death."

Answer: "I remembered his birthday, but cannot remember the other things."

Q: "How old was he, that is, how much older than you was he?"

A: "I don't know. I can remember my grandfather's date of birth because his birthday was the day before mine, and when he turned sixty I turned six. I've never forgotten that!"

Q: "Were your father and mother the same age?"

A: "Why, no. He was two and a half years older than she was."

Q: "You don't know when she was born."

A: "No, she never seemed to tell anyone about her age."

Q: "How old was your mother when she married?"

A: "She was seventeen, but she didn't want me to marry when I was seventeen!"

Q: "Your parents married in 1907, so your mother was born in either 1889 or 1890?"

A: "That must be right."

Q: "Your parents married in November of 1907 and your mother's birthday was in March, so she would have been seventeen in March of 1907."

A: "Yes, she must have been born in March of 1890."

Q: "Your father's birthday was November 7th?"

A: "That's right."

Q: "And he was two and one-half years older than your mother?"

A: "Yes."

Q: "So he must have been born in 1887."

A: "Yes, that's right."

Q: "How old was your father when he died?"

A: "I really don't remember."

Q: "Do you remember any birthday parties before he died, with lots of candles on the cake?"

A: "He always liked birthday parties, but not for himself. As a matter of fact, I think he passed not long before a birthday."

Q: "What was the weather like the day he passed away?"

A: "It was beautiful, the last warm day of Indian summer. It was cold and windy the day of his funeral."

Q: "Did your father live long enough to see all of his grandchildren?"

A: "Oh, yes. He even saw the first grandchild, his great-grandchild."

Q: "But not the second?"

A: "That's right."

Thus interviewing can lead to more details by making the subject think not of remembering specific data but of surrounding incidents. If the subject of the interview was born in 1908, married in 1927, had her first child in 1928, her first grandchild in 1950 and her second in 1952, the date of her father's death has been narrowed considerably. This can lead to checking the town newspaper for an obituary. It there is not enough time for this before publication, it could be noted that the father of the subject died between 23 July 1950 and 5 March 1952, probably in October.

The obvious problem with interviewing by correspondence is that you cannot always anticipate the direction that an answer might lead future questioning. However, if questions are kept short, with a space following each one for a brief reply, and there are not many questions, an answer may be forthcoming promptly, allowing further questions to be sent within a short time.

Tape recorded interviews are the most valuable. Not only do they permit the completion of notes after the interview is over, but they make a prized family memento. During the recording it is often helpful to take notes which will guide the line of inquiry, but full notes, perhaps even a transcript, can be made later. A copy should be sent to the subject for verification. While this is being done it may be possible to check records and determine whether the answers given from memory correspond with the facts. It is a courtesy, if you plan to quote from a tape recording, to allow the subject to edit, and even change, the wording in the transcript. An amended transcript is still quotable. Not only will the relatives appreciate this courtesy, but a look at the transcript may jog the memory even more, and also be an encouragement to buy the book.

The telephone is a very useful tool, and many genealogical and city libraries have a good collection of current or recent directories, perhaps international in scope. The value of using foreign directories may be great, or relatively little. Telephone service is not spread as widely in most countries as it is in the United States and Canada. Many people are simply not listed. Furthermore, mailing addresses may not always be apparent from directory listings, and a call may reveal that the two people trying to communicate may have no language in common. It is much harder to speak and understand a foreign language over the phone than it is to a person in the same room. Nonetheless, international direct dialing is now with us, and calls, if kept short, are not too expensive.

Once the questionnaires and interviews are completed it may be obvious that you have a great deal of material. Not all of the data need be used. For example, if a subject put down his education as having attended Valley School through the fourth grade it might be helpful to simply state that he attended Valley School.

In any event, the circulation of the first typed draft, in photocopy form, to the included relatives is wise. They should be asked for corrections. There may not be any forthcoming, but they will be thinking about buying the book.

Please fill in this form as completely as possible. Estimate dates where not definitely known, but always mark estimates with a question mark or remarks explaining them.

Full name of subject_____

Address_____

Place of birth_____

Date of birth_____

Place of marriage_____

Date of marriage_____

Name of church, minister, etc._____

Place of death_____

Date of death_____

Place of burial_____

Religious preference_____

Occupation_____

Spouse's occupation_____

Military service record (either)_____

Titles of publications (either)_____

Other marriages (subject and/or spouse)_____

Education: School(s)_____

   Degree(s), Date(s)_____

Spouse's education_____

Children: Give full first and middle names, place and date of birth, and mailing address; or, if deceased, give all data on this and attached sheet(s).

1.
_____

2.
_____

3.
_____

4.
_____

5.
_____

6.
_____

7.
_____

Check here if additional data on other side of this sheet_____

Check here if additional sheets are used_____

Please return this form to:

Full (maiden) name of subject's spouse _____
Address _____
Place of birth _____
Date of birth _____
Place of death _____
Date of death _____
Place of burial _____
Full name of spouse's father _____
Place, date of birth _____
Place, date of marriage _____
Place, date of death _____
Place of burial _____
Spouse's paternal grandfather _____
Place, date of birth _____
Place, date of marriage _____
Place, date of death _____
Spouse's paternal grandmother _____
Place, date of birth _____
Place, date of death _____
Full maiden name of spouse's mother _____
Place, date of birth _____
Place, date of death _____
Place of burial _____
Spouse's maternal grandfather _____
Place, date of birth _____
Place, date of marriage _____
Place, date of death _____
Spouse's maternal grandmother _____
Place, date of birth _____
Place, date of death _____
Additional data or comments (if information is from any
printed source or old manuscript give bibliographical data—
full name(s) of author(s), full title, publisher, place and date
of publication, page numbers, etc. — use other side of sheet
if necessary). Give additional biographical data, anecdotes,
etc.

WRITING THE DRAFT

If you do not already have a good typewriter with a carbon ribbon, or a computer with a letter quality printer, the point at which you are ready to type the first draft is the time to make a decision. It is time to buy, rent, lease or borrow a machine which may not only use carbon ribbons, but perhaps a correcting ribbon as well. Cloth ribbons should never be used when producing camera-ready copy. The quality of the typing is very important; it is the very first thing to be noticed by the reader, and insofar as it is an example of your attention to detail it reflects upon the quality of your scholarship.

In addition to the carbon ribbon, interchangeable type is an important feature to be sought. Whether the type is on an element shaped like a ball or a wheel may not be important, but interchangeability is. Much of this compiler's work was typed on an IBM Selectric which was purchased new and was fifteen years old and had been used to produce millions of words before it was placed in semi-retirement in favor of an Eagle computer and a NEC printer. The typewriter was expensive, but required a minimum of maintenance over the years. Elements used have included the Adjutant 12 for normal book face, a trilingual library type used to provide a variety of foreign language accent marks and the symbol for the British pound, an Italic courier 12 type used where italics were required, and an element called Symbol 12, which contains various symbols and supernumerals of value, including vertical lines, some accent marks and Greek letters.

Type is less easily changed on a thimble or daisy wheel computer printer. However, the NEC thimble used in the production of earlier editions of this work contained more characters than will be found on a typewriter, even if to use some of them long codes must be typed within the text. This fourth edition was produced on a GoldStar 286 computer with an HP Laser printer.

Typewriter and computer dealers can provide catalogs of available typefaces, and these should be sought prior to the decision to purchase, or even rent or lease. A typeface suitable for correspondence will not necessarily be appropriate for the production of a book. Thus it may be helpful to compare the type catalogs with books of a general nature printed in type found pleasing to the eye. Genealogical journals are another excellent source of ideas.

Correcting ribbons are relatively recent in their application, but will be available on an increasing number of used typewriters. Many find the correcting ribbon to be much superior to the use of correction fluid, such as Liquid Paper, which is also expensive. Unless you are a professional typist it is likely there will be a need to correct many mistakes. With a correcting ribbon you simply hit the backspace correction key, type the error once again, then type the corrected letter and go on. When using the fluid, you must shift the element away from the area of the mistake, shake the bottle of fluid with vigor, open the bottle, check to see that the right amount of fluid is on the brush, apply the fluid carefully so that it covers the mistake but does not spread too much or gum the paper, replace the brush in the bottle with care, make sure the cap is tight, return the element to the correct position, blow on the fluid if it is not dry, and then type the correction. Liquid Paper, carefully applied, is in some ways superior, but the ribbons are generally most adequate and easy to use. The difference between a correction ribbon and correcting tape is that the ribbon lifts the error off the paper while the tape covers the error with another layer of white, which tends to make the subsequent typing uneven.

Many brands of typewriters can be purchased in local outlets, new or used. As one looks at the available machines it becomes obvious that there are a number of features to be considered, such as the width of the carriage, the availability of repeating keys and other offerings. It might be wise, if you are familiar with the standard keyboard, to order a typewriter with the keyboard marked for use with something other than the normal element. This typist used a standard element or thimble most of the time, but found the international keyboard to be very useful in finding quickly the variety of accents marks placed in unfamiliar locations on a trilingual element. Most features should be selected according to personal taste, and perhaps the nationality of one's ancestors, but a wide carriage will always prove useful, particularly in typing pedigree charts. Inexperienced typists should consider looking for a machine with a Dvorak, rather than standard (or QWERTY) keyboard.

Unfortunately you must use caution when buying used equipment as many stolen items are for sale. Some manufacturers provide a service checking the serial numbers of used machines against a "hot list." In general, if the seller can provide an original bill of sale or evidence that the equipment has been serviced by a manufacturer's representative, it is safe to buy it. Even reputable dealers have been found with stolen typewriters for sale, so great caution must be exercised.

Once the typewriter or computer and printer have been acquired and a supply of paper suitable for typing camera-ready copy have been purchased, the typing of drafts can begin. Local stationers and printers can advise concerning the appropriate paper. Should one use pica or elite type, or perhaps both, as will be allowed by newer machines?

Considerable thought should be given to the ultimate size of the book, the amount of reduction to be used in the printing of it, and the format.

Most genealogies are either eight and one-half by eleven, six by nine, or five and one-half by eight and one-half inches in size. The larger size may prove to be desirable if a number of large photographs, such as family group portraits, are planned for inclusion. The camera-ready copy of such a quarto format can be typed on eight and one-half by eleven inch stock using one inch margins all around. The copy would then be printed at 100%, meaning that the type is not reduced at all. Since a line of type six and one-half inches long contains seventy-eight elite characters, any reduction in printing would make scanning the page difficult for a reader with good eyesight, and nearly impossible for a reader with vision problems. The per page cost of having a quarto volume printed is about double the cost of a five and one-half by eight and one-half inch book, however.

While the smaller octavo book is the cheapest common size to manufacture, it is too small for the purpose of producing a family history, which must be large enough to allow considerable indentation of the data on the children of a couple. Thus you should consider the most viable alternative to the large format, which is the six by nine page. The manufacturing cost of this medium format is about ten per cent higher than the smaller size, but also about forty-five per cent cheaper than the large page book.

This volume is an example of a six by nine inch format with the type reduced by the book manufacturer during the process of making negatives. The camera-ready copy was typed on a GoldStar 286 computer using WordPerfect 5.0 software. The copy is typed and then formatted for printing later in lines 5.3 inches wide, for eventual reduction by the book manufacturer's camera to 88% of the original size. The amount of reduction of any book with typed copy can be measured by the reader by comparing the number of lines printing within perhaps five vertical inches against the number, thirty, originally produced. Pica type can be reduced more than elite type, and margins of less than one inch are appropriate for the six by nine volume, so you will not suffer a significant reduction in the number of words per page by planning for the smaller format.

While the amount of reduction is an important factor in cutting the number of pages in a volume, and thus reducing costs, the printed type should generally be about 90% of the size of the original. When this compiler began typing the final copy of *Ancestral Lines Revised* (1981), however, it was determined that a figure of 83% would be necessary, for even at that size the book was still 666 pages long. A short work might best be produced at 100%, or perhaps even 110%, of the original size. Whatever the change, it will have no bearing on the cost beyond that incurred for manufacturing a specific number of pages of a particular size.

Once you have inspected a number of family histories, it will be possible to select an example which is pleasing, and this will help to determine the format and extent of reduction. When this compiler was considering reduction he looked at the clearly typed copy in George McCracken's *The American Genealogist.* Aware that Dr. McCracken typed his copy on an IBM Selectric, which like most machines types six lines per inch, the compiler was able to measure the reduction. As the printed copy measured eight lines per inch it was obvious that the reduction was to 75%. This was possible because Dr. McCracken used pica type for the major portions of the text, and elite type only for data concerning children and for footnotes. A machine which can type in two different sizes is said to use "dual pitch."

Drafts should always be typed with the margins set as if the final camera-ready copy were being produced. The top and bottom margins are not critical in the draft stage unless one is seeking a precise idea of the number of pages in the final work, and some genealogists may even wish to type the initial drafts doublespaced to allow easier proofreading and marking of errors. Corrections to the drafts should be made in ink, preferably with a fine tipped pen, as pencil will smear over the years you are working on a volume.

Preliminary decisions having been made, it becomes necessary to work out the details of the typing format. Following is an example of material taken from current drafts of a projected third edition of *Ancestral Lines,* which is then discussed point by point below.

HOWLAND

Despite the fact that much effort was expended in research into the question of the parentage of the Howland immigrants, it was not documented until 1937. Previously the parents were said to have been from Essex, and it should be noted that Humphrey Howland's wife was buried in Barking, Essex, where, it is possible, the family may have had more than casual ties. Further information, however, might best be gleaned from the Bishops' Transcripts of Fen Stanton, Huntingtonshire, which date back to 1599. In addition, local records in Newport and Wicken in Essex should be checked [see Crapo, 141-154]. Mary Brown Bonney has been most helpful with this line.

A.   HENRY HOWLAND lived in Fen Stanton, Huntingtonshire, England, in 1629, and was buried there 19 May 1635 [Torrey, *TAG*, 14:214-215].

His wife Margaret was buried at Fenton Stanton 31 July 1629 [*Howland Quarterly*, 28:6]. Henry's son Humphrey gave to his daughter Anne all the pewter marked "A. H." which had belonged to her grandmother, so it would appear that Henry had an earlier wife. It has been said by Leon C. Hill that he married at St. Mary's, Ely, Cambridgeshire, England, 26 April 1600, Alice Aires. Sir Anthony Wagner, Garter King of Arms, has stated that the Henry who married Alice Aires was a different man [*Ibid.*]. Moreover, this marriage is not found in the extant parish registers, so confirmation would have to be sought in the Bishops' Transcripts [Hunt]. In any event, Alice Aires could not have been the mother of John[1] Howland, who was born in 1592.

Nothing further has been discovered concerning Henry Howland, except for the data concerning his children, much of which was found in the records of the Drapers' Company of London.

He was an ancestor of a number of famous people, some of whom have been noted in the text under his sons.

Children, order uncertain:

1.   i.   Arthur[1], bur. Marshfield, Plymouth Colony, 30 Oct. 1675; m. Mrs. Margaret (--) Walker.

2.   ii.   John, d. Plymouth, Plymouth Colony, 23 Feb. 1672/3; m. Elizabeth[2] Tilley.

iii.   Margaret, m. Fen Stanton 26 April 1623 Richard Phillips of Fen Stanton, shoemaker.

iv.   Humphrey, b. c. 1599; bur. St. Swithin's, London, 9 July 1646; m. (1) St. Mary's, White Chapel, co. Middlesex, 21 Nov. 1622, Margaret Calvert, m. (2) Oct. 1636 Anne (Mary), who bur. Barking, Essex, 20 Dec. 1653.

He was appointed to James Smith of the Drapers' Company of London 19 Nov. 1613, and made free 1 Dec. 1620. Of St. Swithin's parish [Lincoln, 93], he left a will dated 28 May 1646, which was proven 10 July 1646. His widow, Anne, was named administratrix of George Howland's estate the next day. Her will, dated 10 Dec. 1653, was proven 22 Nov. 1654 by one William Courtoyse.

v.   George, d. 10 Feb. 1643/4 [Pilgrim John Howland Society]; of the parish of St. Dunstan's in east London [F. Howland, 18], he was described as a London merchant in a bill filed 24 Dec. 1644 by Humphrey Howland of

London, draper, "brother and administrator of the of the goods of George Howland, against Nathaniel Withers of London, merchant."

    vi. Simon, bapt. 19 August 1604; apprenticed to Humphrey Howland in 1622/3 and made free 24 March 1629.

3. vii. Henry, d. Plymouth Colony 17 March 1671; m. Mary.

1. ARTHUR[1] HOWLAND, born in England, was buried in Marshfield, Plymouth Colony, 30 Oct. 1675 [McCracken, *NEHGR*, 104:221; Sherman's *Vital Records Marshfield*, 9].

He married Mrs. Margaret (--) Walker, who was buried in Marshfield 22 Jan. 1683 [Wakefield, *NGSQ*, 71:84], and had a son, John Walker, by an earlier marriage, who married in Marshfield, 20 Oct. 1654, Lydia Reed.

After Arthur Howland's arrival in Plymouth Colony about 1633 [Anderson's *Smith-Hale*, 462], he lived in Plymouth and Marshfield, buying 300 acres from William Partridge for £21, of which £13 was paid in money and the rest in corn and cattle.

In 1640 he was granted fifty acres of land "and some meddow" at the North River. He was a member of the Society of Friends and apparently he regularly "entertayned the forraigne Quakers who were goeing too & frow in some of the townes of the goument, producing great disturbance." On Monday 21 Dec. 1657 the town constable, John Phillips, tried to arrest him and Robert Huchin, a foreign Quaker (that is, not of the town), but Arthur Howland, then aged about 70, threw Phillips out of his house. Surrendering the next day, he refused to post bond and was imprisoned. While in jail he wrote a letter to the General Court, which met 2 March 1658 and held that the letter, "on the pusing therof, appeered to be full of factiouse, seditious, slanderouse passages, to be of dangerouse consequence," so that he was sentenced by the Court to pay £5 for resisting the constable and to post a surety bond for his future good behavior. He refused to post this bond, and to pay a £4 fine instead, so stayed in jail until 1 June 1658, when his release was allowed, "considering his age and infeirmities," by the court, of which his brother John was a member. He and his wife were fined 10/- for absenting themselves from worship in 1658, and in October 1669 he was prosecuted for not paying his share of the minister's rate.

His will, dated 3 July 1675, was proven 7 March 1675/6. Her will, dated 19 Jan. 1683, was proven 5 March 1683/4, the inventory having been appraised 25 Jan. 1683/4 [Wakefield, *NGSQ*, 71:85].

Winston Churchill was a descendant in the tenth generation [*NYGBR*, 73:161].

Children, his, born in Marshfield, only the last certainly of the marriage of Arthur and Margaret:

    *   i. Deborah^2, m. 4 Jan. 1648/9 Lt. John^1 Smith.

        ii. Mary, d. Marshfield 26 August 1690; m. (1) 6 June 1653 Timothy^1 Williamson, m. (2) 22 Jan. 1679/80 Robert Stan[d]ford.

     iii. Martha, d. Hingham, Mass., 19 Dec. 1732; m. (1) 15 March 1659 John Damon of Scituate, m. (2) Hingham 19 Feb. 1679/80 Peter Bacon.

     iv. Elizabeth, m. John Low.

      v. Arthur, m. 9 Dec. 1667 Elizabeth^2 Prence.

    2. JOHN^1 HOWLAND, born in England perhaps in 1592, died in Plymouth, Plymouth Colony, 23 Feb. 1672/3, aged about 80, and was buried there two days later, probably on his own land.

He married in Plymouth, about 1624 (the date 14 August 1623 having been given without documentation by one compiler), Elizabeth^2 Tilley*, who died in Swansea, Plymouth Colony, at the home of her daughter Lydia (Howland) Brown, 21 Feb. 1687/8, aged 80, her will, dated 17 Dec. 1686, giving her age as 79.

He came to Plymouth on the *Mayflower* in 1620. En route he was swept overboard in a heavy sea, but was able to hold onto some halliards and be rescued with the aid of a boat hook. He was thirteenth of the forty-one signers of the Mayflower Compact on 21 Nov. 1620, and was in the party which had the first encounter with the Indians at Great Meadow Creek three days before most of the passengers landed at Plymouth.

He had come to Plymouth as a "servant" to Governor John Carver, although it is obvious that his station in life was somewhat higher than that of the usual servant, for when Governor and Mrs. Carver both died in the spring of 1621, leaving no children of their own, they apparently left him their estate [Willison, 443]. Left in the Carver household after that first terrible winter were John Howland, Desire Minter (a girl of about 21 from Leyden in the Netherlands), Elizabeth Tilley, who was about 14 or 15 and had been taken in by the Carvers upon the deaths of her own parents a couple of months before, and "the boy" William Latham. Desire Minter was apparently hostess of the house for a time, but returned to England within a few years. John and Elizabeth named their first child after her.

He had a house on First Street, Plymouth, and later acquired four acres on Watson's Hill in Plymouth as well as considerable acreage in Duxbury and Rocky Nook, now Kingston.

The settlement at Plymouth was responsible to the London Company for providing a return on the stockholders' investment in settling the *Mayflower* passengers in America. The communal system in use for a few years after 1620 had not resulted in the necessary productivity, and, as private enterprise was not possible under the terms of the colony's relationship with the company, in 1626 and 1627 William Brewster, William Bradford, Edward Winslow, Miles Standish, Thomas Prence, John Alden, Isaac Allerton and John Howland became purchasers and undertakers, that is, they purchased the colony's freedom from the London Company and undertook to settle the colony's debt. As a part of the project to raise the money needed to pay the debt over a fifteen year period, Howland became the commander of a Pilgrim trading post at Kennebec, now Augusta, Maine [Willison, 263].

In April of 1634 a prominent citizen of Massachusetts Bay, John Hocking, established a post north of that of the Pilgrims, cutting off a large part of their lucrative beaver trade. Howland, as commander, led a group including Thomas Savory and Moses Talbot to protest to Hocking, who held a gun first at Savory's head and then at Talbot's as they argued. In the hearing following the incident it was said that Howland told Hocking to point the gun at him, as commander, if he felt that he had to be prepared to shoot someone, but Hocking shot Moses Talbot in the head at close range and was himself shot and killed by someone on the Pilgrims' boat [F. Howland, 317-318].

He served as Assistant to the Governor from 1633 to 1635, and as a Committeeman or Deputy to the General Court in 1637, 1639-1652, 1659, 1661-1668 and 1670. He was a Selectman of Plymouth in 1666, and often served on committees appointed to "lay out and appraise land, run out highways," and settle petty disputes [F. Howland, 317]. He was the last surviving passenger of the *Mayflower* to live in the Town of Plymouth, although others survived longer in the western parts of the colony. He was an ancestor (at the eighth generation) of President Franklin Delano Roosevelt. His will was dated 29 May 1672.

Children, listed in his will, born in Plymouth:

    i. Desire[2], b. 1625; d. Barnstable, Plymouth Colony, 13 Oct. 1683; m. 1643 John[2] Gorham.

    ii. John, b. 24 Feb. 1626/7; m. West Barnstable 26 Oct. 1651 Mary[2] Lee.

    iii. Hope, b. 30 (or 3?) August 1629; d. 8 March 1684/5 (or in Barnstable, 8 Jan. 1683/4 [Pilgrim John Howland Society]); m. 1646 John[1] Chipman, son of Thomas Chipman.

    iv. Elizabeth, d. Oyster Bay, Long Island; m. (1) Plymouth 13 Sept. 1649 Ephraim[2] Hicks, m. (2) Plymouth 10 July 1651 John Dickinson.

*   v. Lydia, m. James[2] Brown.

*   vi. Hannah, m. Rehoboth 6 July 1661 Jonathan[3] Bosworth.

    vii. Ruth, m. Plymouth 17 Nov. 1664 Thomas[3] Cushman.

    viii. Joseph, d. 1704; m. Plymouth 7 Dec. 1664 Elizabeth[2] Southworth.

    ix. Jabez, d. Bristol, R. I.; m. Bethiah[2] Thacher.

    x. Isaac, b. 15 Nov. 1649; d. Middleboro, Mass., 9 March 1723/4; m. Elizabeth Vaughn, daughter of George Vaughn.

3.   HENRY[1] HOWLAND, born in England, was a resident of Plymouth Colony when he died 17 March 1671.

His wife, Mary, died 17 August 1674; there is no proof her surname was Newland.

He was apprenticed to his brother Humphrey of the Drapers' Company of London 1 Oct. 1623, but, it seems, did not complete his apprenticeship. It is said his first mention in the Plymouth records was in the allotment of cattle to different families in 1624 as the owner of a "black cow," but it should be remembered that if he did begin his apprenticeship at the usual age he was still under eighteen years of age at this time.

He was named freeman in Plymouth in 1633, probably shortly after he established himself on his own. On 25 March of that year he was taxed 9/-, payable at 6/- per bushel of corn. The following year he was taxed 18/-.

He was among the earliest settlers of Duxbury, "by the bay side, near Love Brewster's," and on 5 Jan. 1635/6 he was chosen constable there. In 1640 he purchased five acres of land and one acre of meadow for twelve bushels of Indian corn. He was surveyor of highways for several years and he served on the Grand Inquest (grand jury) in 1636, 1637, 1639, 1640, 1649, 1651-1653 and 1656, refusing to serve in 1657 due to his having become a Quaker [F. Howland, 63-64n]. He was fined for the first time for entertaining Quakers in 1657, in October. It is possible that he began to lean towards Quaker beliefs as early as 1651, for in 1652 he and others obtained a large tract of land along the western borders of the colony, now Dartmouth, where, it was agreed, Quakers could live in peace.

On 2 April 1659 he and twenty-six others purchased land now part of Freetown, Mass., from Wamsutta and Pattapanum. He was granted land also in Bridgewater, and in 1664 bought land in Mettapoisett, now Swansea, Mass.

He was an ancestor of Presidents Nixon and Ford [*TAG*, 61:178]. His will, dated 28 Nov. 1670, was proven 8 March 1671/2, while his wife's will was dated 8 May 1674 and proven 8 April 1675.

Children, the first two born in Duxbury:

      i. Joseph², d. 15 August 1692; m. 4 May 1683 Rebecca Huzzey of Hampton, N. H., who m. (2) Samuel Collins of Lynn, Mass.

4.   ii. Zoeth, d. 21 Jan. 1676; m. Dec. 1656 Abigail, who m. (2) 2 Feb. 1678/9 Richard² Kirby.

   iii. John, d. c. 1687; unm.; lived Freetown.

   iv. Samuel, d. 1716; m. Mary.

   v. Sarah, m. 16 Jan. 1672 Robert Dennis of Portsmouth.

   vi. Elizabeth, m. 1691 Jedediah² Allen.

   vii. Mary, m. James Cudworth of Duxbury.

   viii. Abigail, d. 7 April 1692; m. 2 Nov. 1678 John Young.

4.   ZOETH² HOWLAND, born in Duxbury, Plymouth Colony, was killed by Indians during King Philip's War at "Pocaset," Rhode Island, 28 March 1676 [inventory].

Friends' Records at Newport, R. I., contain the following: "Zoar Howlan of Dartmouth in plimoth Colony was maried to Abigall his wife in the tenth month [Dec.] of the year one thousand six hundred fifty-six." She married second, 2 Feb. 1678, Richard² Kirby. He took the oath of fidelity at Duxbury in 1657 but was fined in December of that year for holding Friends' Meeting in his house. In March of 1657/8 he and Abigail were sentenced to sit in the stocks for an hour "for speaking opprobiously of the minnesters of Gods Word," and it is believed he moved to Dartmouth as early as 1662.

At the time of his death in King Philip's War he owned only "I quarter hsare of land valued att 15=0=0." The total inventory of his estate was £36.14s.6d.

Children, the first eight recorded in Newport Friends records:

5.   i. Nathaniel³, b. Duxbury 5 August 1657; d. Dartmouth 3 May 1723; m. 1684 Rose⁴ Allen.

   ii. Benjamin, b. 8 March 1659; d. 12 April 1727; m. 23 June 1684 Judith Sampson.

   iii. Daniel, b. July 1661; m. Mary Sampson [Wilbour's *Little Compton Families*, 353].

   iv. Lydia, b. 23 Sept. 1663.

   v. Mary, b. 23 Dec. 1665.

    vi. Sarah, b. Feb. 1668.

   vii. Henry, b. 30 June 1672; m. (1) 3 June 1698 Deborah Briggs, m. (2) 12 Feb. 1714 Elizabeth Northupp [Wilbour].

  viii. Abigail, b. 30 June 1672; int. m. 6 Jan. 1700/1 Abraham Booth.

   ix. Nicholas, perhaps m. Hannah Woodman, who b. Dartmouth 27 Jan. 1679.

5. NATHANIEL[3] HOWLAND, born in Duxbury, Plymouth Colony, 5 Oct. 1657, died in Dartmouth, Massachusetts, 3 May 1723.

He married in 1684 Rose[4] Allen.

He served as a selectman of Dartmouth for several terms from 1699, as a member of the grand jury in 1702, and as moderator of the town meeting in 1721. He served on many committees, and was active in Friends Monthly Meeting. He also served as minister of the town.

The inventory of his estate was £1790, plus £530 for his homestead.

Children, recorded in Dartmouth Friends records:

   *   i. Rebeckah[4], b. 25 August 1685; d. 8 Nov. 1727; m. 1709 James[3] Russell.

      ii. John, b. 14 April 1687; d. 1749.

    iii. James, b. 18 Feb. 1689; m. 25 July 1717 Deborah[4] Cook [Wilbour, 254].

    iv. Sarah, b. 15 Nov. 1690; m. 1720 Timothy Akin.

     v. George, b. 4 Dec. 1693; m. Hannah Akin.

    vi. Mary, b. 23 April 1699; m. 1702 Peleg Smith.

   vii. Content, b. 20 August 1702; m. Wesson Briggs of Dartmouth.

In *Ancestral Lines Revised* the Howland material was preceded by the Holzwarth family and following by the Hull line. The Howland family covered 324 lines at sixty-seven characters and spaces per line, but here would have taken about 405 lines at 53 characters per line, to be reduced to 88% in this volume had pica typewriter style type been used, in part because each line in a child's entry contains fewer characters, thus causing a significantly greater number of lines to be generated. However, the 12 point Bitstream Times Roman type used here (and then reduced to 88% of the original size) allowed the same material to be set in 248 lines with an average of about sixty-six characters per line.

The symbol used to separate the families should be selected with care. It should strike once in the center of the page, with the other strikes an equal distance on either side. When using a typewriter this compiler found it easier to insert the paper in the center, and then backspace once for each couple of characters in the family name before typing "Howland." The last dangling character was ignored in backspacing.

For the purpose of consistency in format, each family was provided with an introduction. This can be of any length, and can be used in a variety of ways, to raise questions, critique sources, credit contributors, suggest further avenues of research, and so forth. The introduction can be as long as necessary.

Following the introduction, the first immigrant known member of the line is numbered 1. The inexperienced typist should determine whether the machine being used has a number "1" or whether the lower case "L" should be used. The capital letter "I" is a Roman numeral not to be used here. Note that each person's name should be spelled the way it was found in the records, not necessarily the way the name would be spelled today. Each person is marked by a generation number or letter following the given name[s]. The immigrant ancestor is marked with a raised one by this compiler (no numbers being used in a line for which the immigrant is not known), each member of the second generation by a raised "two", and so forth. This compiler developed the habit of labeling the immigrant's parents with the Greek letter alpha, his or her grandparents with a beta, and so forth, when he was using a Selectric typewriter, and this practice has spread considerably. This is more easily done with a typewriter than with a letter quality printer, however, so when the printer is being used the generation of a pre-immigrant member of the family is simply marked with an upper case letter. If only the father of the immigrant is known, as in the case of the Howland line, the first letter used will be an "A", but if the grandfather is known, the first person will be lettered with a "B", and the next with an "A".

Indenting in a family history or genealogy may be based on twos rather than larger numbers. Small indentations conserve lines, and reduce the number of pages, as well as the expense of publication.

A foreign place of birth may be quoted exactly as given in the source, with the translation to modern spelling given in brackets to denote that this was not in the original quotation. The quoting is done not to be pedantic, but to permit the idea that the name given is not absolutely to be interpreted as the name identified in brackets. Any material in brackets is an addition or alteration to the original. Parentheses are used to repeat material given in parentheses in the original source.

The first paragraph of any entry should generally contain the number "1", or a capital letter if pre-immigrant ancestry is known, followed by the given name[s] of the subject, the generation number (if applicable), the surname as spelled at the time, place of birth, date of birth, place of death, date of death, place and date of burial with supporting details of interest, and perhaps dates of a will or probate records (omitting the contents). One common mistake is to give a place and date of baptism or christening in lieu of birth data, but labeling the date of baptism as the date of birth. In many areas the dates of baptism and burial are easily accessible, and this data may be presented in lieu of missing vital records if properly identified.

The second paragraph will generally give the details of the subject's marriage[s]. A typical form would be, "He/she married in [place], [date], [full name of spouse followed by an asterisk if ancestry given elsewhere in the volume], who [additional details as necessary]." Her/his date of death should be included, if known, along with any details of a will, probate, or letters of administration. One must be careful with syntax in constructing these paragraphs. A sentence reading, "He married in Swansea, 21 June 1695, Mary Jones, daughter of Paul and Elizabeth Jones, who died 17 Nov. 1731," leaves much to be desired. Antecedents must be kept obvious. Who died in 1731, Mary or Elizabeth? Most commonly it would appear that Mary did, but if the syntax has been used correctly the person who died in 1731 was Elizabeth. Thus such data should read, if Mary died in 1731, "He married in Swansea, 21 June 1695, Mary Jones, who died 17 Nov. 1731, and was daughter of Paul and Elizabeth Jones." Never hesitate to repeat the full name of the person for whom additional data is being given.

There may follow any number of paragraphs of a biographical nature, and these may include such criticism of sources or explanation of history as may seem required. Details of wills, probate and the like are perhaps best reserved for the final paragraph of the narrative, prior to the listing of the children.

Hopefully it has been noted that sources in the examples have been given consistently in brackets, rather than in footnotes, the use of supernumerals being reserved solely for indicating the generation number of the family in the country of the compiler, or perhaps from the first known member anywhere. The style of the citation in brackets should permit the reader to turn quickly to the bibliography. The citations should be reasonably clear, but may well assume some knowledge on the part of the reader, as in "[P.C.C. Hogan 27]." There is no harm leaving something for the novice to research, such as the abbreviation for the Prerogative Court of Canterbury. Space in a family history is too valuable to explain each source every time it is mentioned. The casual reader well be advised to skip the citations in brackets, even if they are properly obtrusive, putting forth the sources of evidence in a way much more forceful than footnotes would be.

Following the narrative paragraphs will be a list of children. The heading of "Children, listed in his will, born in Plymouth:" following the material on John[1] Howland, is representative of the usual format to be used. This gives the place of birth (if all were born in the same place); the source of the data may also be included in this line.

The children are then listed in their known or approximate order, or perhaps the order of their listing in probate records. Often the latter type of list presented the sons in order of age and then the daughters, even though a daughter might have been the first born. This was particularly true in England. The heading in such cases might be, "Children, as listed in the probate records."

This compiler has followed the practice of giving the place and date of birth, death and marriage[s] for each child as fully as possible, even when it is repeated elsewhere, out of consideration for researchers who do not wish to photocopy several pages to obtain data for one family group sheet. Certainly baptism and burial data may be given in addition to, or in lieu of, other records, but they should be carefully identified.

The recording of a child's birth in a particular town does not mean the birth took place there. Often the vitals were recorded sometime after the fact, at the convenience of the parents. Many births, many marriages and a few deaths have been recorded in more than one town.

There is some argument over whether each child should be given a small Roman numeral, and whether only those children for whom a line is carried further should be given an Arabic number to the left. Those who favor this system, including the compiler, are attempting to put all Arabic numbers in use consecutively at the beginning of each entry for a "head of household," as he or she might be called, even if female heads listed in a single-family genealogy were not really such. The consecutive use of numbers serves as a check against omitting materials. Those who simply assign an Arabic number to each child state that this allows material to be added easily in its proper order at a later date. That argument does not hold water, however, whenever, as is usually the case, grandchildren are also added.

In a multi-family work, an asterisk in place of an Arabic numeral to the left of the small Roman numeral is an indication that a female child has been treated further within the entry for her husband. Likewise, when a wife is mentioned within a family group, and her name has been followed by an asterisk, her ancestry can be found under her maiden surname. Occasionally it may be necessary to stipulate under which surname one should look, if the wife's maiden name and the usual spelling of the family name are different.

The generation number of a husband and wife will frequently be different. Each number should be based on the number of generations in a direct line from the immigrant ancestor. However, if the ancestry of an immigrant wife of a non-American (or non-Australian as the case may be) ancestor is known, the letters of the wife will be the same as her husband's and the letters for her ancestors will progress in order from hers. Obviously, if there is no asterisk, nothing of the wife's ancestry has been presented in another part of the work.

As an aside, this compiler has employed the practice of including generation numbers whenever the ancestral line of a person was known, even if it was not given in the work being written. This is an indication that some source listed in the bibliography contains the full line to the immigrant.

In the example above, there are several lines of descent given from Henry Howland, through each of three of his sons. The line of descent from Arthur[1] Howland can be followed through the Smith family. Lines of descent from John[1] Howland can be followed through both the Brown and Bosworth families, and the one from Henry[1] Howland can be traced down through a grandson, and then through the Russell family. When there is descent through three sons then each is assigned consecutive Arabic numerals and as one follows the numbers in order he swings from one line to the other and back as he progresses through each generation.

In a single-family genealogy an attempt may be made to trace all of the descendants, or at least those of the same surname, which is generally much more feasible. If tracing all the descendants, one should never assign generation numbers through the female lines, but rather assign them according to the husband's ancestry, if known, or omit them altogether. When tracing families in different countries it may seem worthwhile to assign generation numbers only to those living in the nation of primary concern to the compiler.

The family sections in a family history should always be arranged in alphabetical order by surname, not in any other order which might prove convenient to a compiler but confusing to everyone else. Nor should there be any additional notation of how the family is related to the compiler, which information will prove to be of interest to very few.

Once the genealogical format or scope has been considered, and the size of the camera-ready page has been decided, there remain questions of English usage and standard typing procedures. Above all, family history must be clear in its presentation. If it is not, the reader may wind up singing the old song, "I'm my own Grandpa!" Thus this compiler has given up any pretensions to literary style for the sake of clarity. He has consistently maintained a set, if dry, format, giving certain details in logical order in paragraphs of carefully established form. Paragraphing has been somewhat visual, that is, done in newspaper style in which paragraphs are deliberately kept brief, even if they might logically and grammatically be joined together.

Language usage is important. A good handbook of English may prove useful to any compiler. A dictionary is essential, and, again, must be consulted whenever words are to be hyphenated unless the writer is an expert. The key to receiving great reviews may be the generous use of the words "possibly" and "perhaps," with questions about, and criticism of, the data written into the narrative itself, rather than reserved for brackets, footnotes or notes at the back of the book, where most readers will not see them.

While this volume cannot be a lesson in writing of basic language, the reader must understand that a great deal of what passes for genealogy is truly awful, both in terms of logic and expression. Negative reviews will result from failure to criticize weak sources, from poor English usage, and from any cute variations from accepted standards. Again, when checking over a draft it is a good idea to read the last sentence first. Does it contain a subject, a predicate, and a complete thought? Then read the second to last sentence, and so on. Remember always that your book will long outlive you, and ultimately will enhance or damage your reputation perhaps more than any other fact of your life.

Questions as to spacing, underlining or italics and the like may be resolved through reference to a text on typing or to examples given within this volume, which can be found if one will consult the index. Errors in spacing are all too common, particularly the failure to leave two spaces at the end of every sentence.

The drafts should be kept in alphabetical order by family with the pages of each clearly numbered. When changes are made it is not necessary to retype an entire draft. Changes can be typed on separate pages ("3A" for example), with notations on the older draft directing the typist to these revisions, or perhaps to the file heading to be used when reading a computer disk.

During the draft stage it is imperative that the bibliography be kept current, preferably on file cards, so the final copy can be typed from these cards once their alphabetical order has been double and triple checked. An example of some bibliographical entries follows.

Anderson, Mary Audentia Smith. *Ancestry and Posterity of Joseph Smith and Emma Hale.* Independence, Mo., 1929.

Arnold, James N. *Vital Record of Rhode Island, 1636-1850*, 21 vols. Providence: Narragansett Historical Publishing Company, 1891-1912.

Hall, Newman A. Talbot Notes. MS.

Howland, Franklyn. *History of Arthur, Henry and John Howland and Their Descendants*. New Bedford, Mass., 1885.

Lincoln, William Ensign. *Some Descendants of Stephen Lincoln of Wymondham, England*. Pittsburgh, Pa., 1930.

McCracken, George E. "The Will of Arthur Howland, Senior, of Marshfield," *The New England Historical and Genealogical Register*, 104 (1950), 221-225.

Providence Gazette, 1822.

Sherman, Robert M., and Ruth Wilder Sherman, compilers. *Vital Records of Marshfield, Massachusetts, to the Year 1850*. Society of Mayflower Descendants in the State of Rhode Island, 1970.

Torrey, Clarence Almon. "The Howland Ancestry," *The American Genealogist*, 14 (1937), 214-215.

Wakefield, Robert S., and Robert M. Sherman. "Arthur Howland of Plymouth, Mass., 1640, his wife Margaret (--) Walker, and their Children," *National Genealogical Society Quarterly*, 71 (1983), 84-93.

Wilbour, Benjamin Franklin. "Cemetery Inscriptions in Tiverton, R. I.," *The New England Historical and Genealogical Register*, 117 (1963), 136.

Wilbour, Benjamin Franklin. *Little Compton Families*. Little Compton, R. I.: Little Compton Historical Society, 1967.

Wilbour, Benjamin Franklin. "Parentage of Susanna Wright, wife of Richard Pearce of Portsmouth, R. I.," *The New England Historical and Genealogical Register*, 84 (1930), 427-433.

Willison, George F. *Saints and Strangers*. New York: Reynal & Hitchcock, 1945.

The bibliography is a significant place in which space can be saved by indenting where necessary only two spaces instead of three. In *Ancestral Lines Revised* the use of only one less space for indentation permitted the saving of three lines in typing eleven entries picked at random. However, even if it means using another full line to avoid typing just one character into the margin, the right margin must be held inviolate without exception. If this is not done the typography will appear to be sloppy and reflect poorly on the other aspects of the work.

The examples shown above reflect a variety of bibliographical entries where the author is known. If no author is given, alphabetize according to the first letter of the article. Entries for articles must contain the full name of the article within quotation marks, the name of the periodical, the volume number, the year of publication, and the page numbers. The words "a," "an," and "the" should be ignored for purposes of alphabetizing titles.

A book should be listed by author or editor, followed by a full title, followed by the place of publication, the publisher (exactly as given on the title page), and the year of publication, usually found on the copyright page on the reverse of the title. Books published in a small town need to be identified also by state; in some cases the publisher has not been identified, and it may usually be assumed the volume was published by the compiler.

Arnold's entry shows how a multi-volume work published over a period of years can be handled. Where multiple places of publication are listed on the title page, only one need be listed in the bibliography. You may choose to list the first listed place, or the place closest to your own home.

Manuscript works should also be listed. The location and date of the work may also be identified in a bibliography. The authors of such works might be found in such publications as Mary Keysor Meyer and P. William Filby's *Who's Who in Genealogy & Heraldry*, the first volume of which was published by Gale Research Company late in 1981.

The example of a newspaper, the *Providence Gazette*, shows only the name of the newspaper and the time span of the issues used in the research. If only one issue of the paper was used, the year of that issue would be given in the bibliography. The details of the exact date of the issue, and the page number if necessary, would be given only in the text, within brackets.

An article from a periodical, magazine or journal should include the author[s] (if known), the title of the article, the name of the periodical, the volume number, an appropriate date (usually just a year, but if each issue begins with a fresh page 1 the exact date should be given), and the pages. If an article runs through a number of issues of a journal, the first page of the article can be given with "ff." for "following."

It may prove wise to abbreviate the periodicals, including a key to the abbreviations at the beginning of the bibliography. Acceptable abbreviations can be found in the *Genealogical Periodical Annual Index* or the revised edition of Jacobus' *Index to Genealogical Periodicals*.

Government documents should be listed alphabetically by title (or author, if given, whether it is a person or an agency or committee).

You may have noticed that some sources cited in the Howland entry were not listed in the sample bibliography (while other sources were listed to provide a wider range of examples). Where this compiler had not personally seen the actual source he did not list it.

Once the drafts have been completed and the bibliography cards have been made and checked, the typing of the final copy may begin. If at the time of the beginning of the typing of the final copy all research has been completed, you can simply begin with an odd numbered page, having made allowance for the estimated number of pages to be used for the title, copyright, table of contents and the preface. This first page will not be numbered and the heading line should be left blank, so that if the top margin has been planned at one and three-quarter inches, on the first page it will be that plus the space of two blank lines.

Then you type the name of the first family, properly centered, the introductory comments on that family (having skipped a line between the family name and the introduction), and then the genealogy. The second page of the text will be even numbered (perhaps page 8 or 10 or 12) and be the first page to bear a heading such as this one does. All even numbered pages should be numbered at the left margin, with the title (or short title) centered in the same line.

Once the heading has been typed you simply continue with the text. The third page will be the first odd numbered page with a heading, which should contain the name or names of the family or families mentioned in the two facing pages (the second and third of the text), with the page number at the right margin. When typing these odd numbered pages it may sometimes prove desirable to type the text first to determine precisely what families will be included before doing the heading.

As you continue typing the text, be sure to continue typing the page numbers and headings in a consistent fashion, according to whether it is an odd or even page. It is easy to make mistakes if you are not careful about this. Of course the text can be typed without headings, if space is left on the paper to add them later, but if this is done it will help to mark the tentative page numbers on each sheet with a nonreproducing pencil as you go along. This is the light blue or purple colored pencil, sold in stationery stores, the markings from which will not be picked up in the platemaking process.

At the time this compiler began typing the final copy of *Ancestral Lines Revised*, the work began with the Brown family of Plymouth and Wannamoisett rather than at the beginning, as the data on the Allsop and Boyer families was not complete. The typing continued through about one hundred pages of copy, later numbered from 127 on, before it was time to turn to typing from the beginning. The device used to link the Boyer to the Brown section with the proper spacing was relatively simple. As the compiler's own biography fell near the end of the Boyer section it was written to fill the necessary number of lines. In other areas introductory material may be expanded as necessary to allow a section to fit without an undue amount of white space.

It is remarkable how much an introduction can be expanded with the inclusion of historical narrative explaining the background or circumstances of a family. A major point in typing the drafts is to allow you to measure the number of lines in a given area. While a printer can expand or shrink the number in the typesetting process, those using a typewriter do not have this leeway. In some cases it may be preferable to tighten the writing rather than to expand it. Padded materials often seem to be written sloppily. The editing can be done most effectively if the need is foreseen over a number of pages, so that the changes are not perceptible. Of course the use of a word processing computer simplifies these chores considerably. Nonetheless, be careful not to compromise the integrity of the genealogical data, as opposed to historical or editorial matter.

As soon as final page numbers are being assigned the process of indexing must begin. While this compiler has often been tempted to simply continue the typing of copy (it is, after all, very satisfying to see the final text take shape), if the indexing is not done as copy is typed it will have to be completed all at once, and then the job will seem to be overwhelming. Every family history should be thoroughly indexed, at least by personal names. The addition of a place index will only enhance its value, and warrant further positive comment by reviewers. Invariably, the lack of indexing will be noted in the journals, sharply reducing sales based on response to reviews.

This compiler's method of indexing has evolved from trial and error, and is described here on the assumption that most genealogists will not have a properly programmed computer at hand. Basically, the compiler makes three passes through the text in the process of indexing. The first pass is for the purpose of noting the place names, and goes quickly. The second pass is for the listing of the members of the primary families in each section, and takes longer. The third pass, in which the incidental personal names are taken down, will require much more time.

All indexing done by the compiler is done by making handwritten lists on folded sheets of eight and one-half by eleven inch paper. For the place names a number of sheets are folded in half vertically. As each new colony or state in the United States was found, the name of that state was printed in large block letters at the top of the sheet, and the name of each town was written neatly on the sheet, with page numbers added each time a mention was found. The quality of the handwriting will need to be good throughout, and all names which are rare or spelled in unusual ways should be printed, lest you find it becomes consistently necessary to refer back to the text to check proper spellings while typing the index.

As a compiler works with the text through a number of drafts, many of the towns mentioned a number of times will come to mind, and in the course of putting the names down it is wise to leave ample space so that page numbers can be inserted after the town name as they appear. However, as each sheet is filled it should be cut into slips which are then placed immediately in an envelope labeled with the name of the colony, state or foreign country. Towns in foreign countries should also bear the designation of a province or shire, but will be arranged alphabetically by town rather than separated by state.

As the place names on any given page of text will generally be from only two or three states, the method of using a separate half page for each state does not prove too cumbersome. Even in the case of *Ancestral Lines Revised*, which included place names from every state except Montana, and from thirty-seven foreign nations, the process of writing down the names went easily. Indeed, the sheets were carried around in a briefcase virtually everywhere the compiler went, and much work was done during breaks, between classes, and while waiting for appointments.

Once the place name indexing was completed for all of the copy which had been typed to date, it was time to turn to indexing the primary families. Again sheets were folded in half vertically. Then the name of the first family in the book was printed at the top in large letters. In the case of the work used as an example, the name was ABELL. Each person in the Abell section was then listed, with the page numbers marked. Wives of Abell males were listed with their first, middle and maiden names, the latter in parenthesis. In reality there were no middle names for Abell wives, but had there been they would have been included. Where there was a wife whose marriage to an Abell was her second or third, not only her maiden name would be listed, but each married name prior to the Abell marriage would be given, each one in parenthesis. Where a maiden name or such is not known, dashes were enclosed in parenthesis instead, as (--). Once the primary lists for the Abell section were completed they were cut apart, leaving little strips with first and middle names, as well as page numbers, for the males, and first, middle, maiden and earlier married names, as well as page numbers, for the females. None of the strips contained the surname Abell. These were promptly put into an envelope marked "Abell" which was then placed in a shoe box, which was kept in a place where it could not be upset by the dog or any of the three cats in the house.

Then it was time to turn to the secondary families in the Abell section, the mention of those people with surnames other than Abell. Again sheets were folded vertically. Any person whose last name began with the letters A through L was listed on the left side, and those M-Z were listed on the right. A further division was made, with those A-D listed from the top left, those E-L from the bottom left going up the sheet, those M-R from the top right, and those from S through Z listed upwards from the bottom right. All people in the Abell section who had a surname other than Abell were listed, surname first, then first (and middle) name, and maiden name, the latter in parenthesis. These included listings for Abell-born females who married men from other families. Thus each female was listed under her maiden name and each of her married names.

These sheets for the secondary families were saved until there were several to be sorted at one time, and then cut into quarters. All the A-D quarters were cut into slips which contained a surname, other marks and page numbers, and these were sorted into envelopes marked A, B, C and D. This process was carried through the alphabet. Once the slips were all made it was time to sort the A envelope by surname, gathering together all the Abells from throughout the remainder of the book, putting them into the Abell envelope, and so on. Of course there were many slips for families not treated as primary ones, and other envelopes had to be used. Ultimately hundreds of envelopes and several shoe boxes proved to be necessary.

The greatest of care was taken to continually check that the A-D, E-L, M-R, and S-Z divisions were constantly maintained. Once the slips had been sorted into the envelopes it was time to dump the contents onto a table secure from dog, cats and breezes, and begin the final sort. At this time the spelling variants of the same name were grouped under the most common spelling, with the other spellings noted as the slips were placed on paper sheets and taped down in order, using a type of transparent tape upon which you can write, and thus readied for typing.

Not until every slip was arranged for the letters A-D, and reread for correct alphabetical order, did the typing of the index begin.

Index work is very tedious, but the task can be made much less so by doing it as one types the final copy. As some of the letter envelopes began to bulge, it proved helpful to sort them further, making envelopes for AB, AC, AD and so forth as the need arose. Taking everything in small steps helps to relieve the boredom of sorting, taping and the like. On the other hand, the typing of the final index is fun, for at that point you can see how close you are getting to publishing.

Examples of index work in final form are to be found in the appendices to this work. An attractive layout is achieved by determining in advance the number of columns to be typed. You must remember that if there are two columns there will be only one column of blank space between the two, while of there are three columns of names there will be two columns of blank space, and so on. In *Ancestral Lines Revised* each line contained sixty-seven characters and spaces. Since about twenty characters per column were desired in the index, the number 67 was divided by three, leaving 22-1/3. Since a blank space could not be the width of two and one-third characters, it was decided to use three equal columns of twenty-one plus two blank columns of two characters each. If each line is sixty characters wide, you could use three eighteen character columns separated by two blank columns of three character width. The given names should be indented not more than two spaces, perhaps one. In any event, the columns of typing must be equal, and the integrity of the margins meticulously maintained.

Of course much of what had been outlined in the preceding paragraphs could be simplified by the use of a computer. However, indexing entirely by computer means not being able to work on the project when you are away from the keyboard. In addition the cost of extra memory and programs for sorting massive amounts of data might not be justified by the time savings on one project. If you want to consider using a computer to do an index, list by hand the names and page numbers from a token number of pages, find an average of the number of characters and spaces to index one page, multiple by the number of pages expected to be in the text, and start talking to knowledgeable software salespeople, specifying the size of your project.

While this chapter has been devoted to the preparation of draft and camera-ready copies, you would be wrong to assume that having followed this work to conclusion you are ready to be publish. If a systems approach has not been followed, as outlined in the next chapter, completion of the final copy will still leave you months away from having the ability to send the material to the book manufacturer.

THE SYSTEMS APPROACH TO PUBLICATION

As you approach completion of the final camera-ready copy of a work it will be obvious that your tasks are far from finished. If every step is completed in a logical, orderly fashion, much time will be saved. If not, months will be lost.

Much must be done: mailing lists, requests for bids from book publishers or manufacturers, arrangements for copyright and listing in *Books in Print*, the placing of ads, and the like. Much of the final effort can be reserved until you are concentrating on the index. You will have to have something else to think about besides this task, the completion of which will take much time. However, the worst you can do is to wait until the book finished and ready for the manufacturer before attending to these other details.

A mailing list can be compiled from the moment the book is planned. It should list the names and addresses of all living relatives mentioned in the book, genealogists with whom you have corresponded about the project, reviewers who might be interested in receiving a review copy of the work, and people noted from the periodical literature and surname directories who may be interested in at least several of the surnames mentioned in your work as primary families. These lists can be kept on file cards and later typed on labels available at stationery stores, available by the sheet or in boxes as large as 3,300; those planning to make several mailings will find that a computer will save a lot of work. Book dealers should also be included, although relatively few of them are interested in a genealogy or family history.

Other tasks will have to wait until the estimated time of completion of work can be determined with some accuracy. However, at least two months before the book will be finished you should write to two offices in the Library of Congress. First, write to the Library of Congress, Cataloging in Publication Program, Washington, DC 20540, and request instructions and an application form for a preassigned Library of Congress Catalog Card Number for your work in progress. Second, write to the United States Copyright Office, Library of Congress, Washington, DC 20559, and request instructions for obtaining a copyright and a copy of Form TX.

At the same time you should write to ISBN U. S. Agency, R.R. Bowker/Martindale-Hubbell at 121 Chanlon Road, New Providence, NJ 07974 (current temporary telephone number [201] 464-6800), requesting assignment of an International Standard Book Number. They will need to know how many books you may intend to publish during your lifetime.

Once the application for an L. C. Catalog Card Number has been received the instructions should be read and followed carefully, and the application filed immediately. It is permissible to estimate the data requested on the form insofar as the number of pages and the publication date are concerned. Once the Library of Congress has provided the number it will be time to make up a mock title page and copyright page. The International Standard Book Number provided by R.R. Bowker in response to completion of their forms should be added to the copyright page. In addition, the makeup of the spine stamp should be considered. If the title on the spine is to be read vertically, it should be positioned so that when the book is laid flat on its back the type will read right side up.

Most local printers are prepared to do this typesetting or to forward orders to someone who does. At the time the order is being discussed with the printer you must know how wide and deep the coverage will be on the camera-ready copy. Thus if the typewritten pages have coverage five inches wide and eight inches deep the title and copyright pages should not exceed this, for they will normally be reduced the same amount as the text in the process of book manufacturing. The printer should have examples of type faces at hand, so you can make an intelligent choice. It is wise not only to specify the type style, but also to provide the typesetter with a mock layout of the pages involved so they can be laid out precisely as they will be sent to the book manufacturer. The title and copyright pages of this book contain the necessary parts. You must proofread the finishing typesetting with extreme care before accepting it.

The instructions for obtaining a copyright, and the Form TX, should be reviewed upon receipt, and, if the Form TX proves to be the appropriate one, this material should be filed for use the day the books are received from the book publisher or manufacturer.

At about the same time you write to the Library of Congress, it would be wise to begin to solicit bids from book publishers or manufacturers for the printing and binding of the completed work. Publishers are more expensive than manufacturers. Publishers also offer services critically needed by the majority of genealogists, who have no wish to spend weeks working to master a few of the facets of the publishing business in order to save some money publishing one book. Book manufacturers are cheaper, but their services vary greatly; some will offer no advice and answer few questions.

This compiler has had considerable contact with Ann Hege Hughes of Gateway Press, 1001 North Calvert Street, Baltimore, MD 21202, largely as a result of recommendations from several readers of the first of edition of this book. She is a lady with an intense personal interest in genealogy whose mission is to work with authors and compilers until their efforts are published. She will assist with individual consultations, book design, the preparation of camera-ready copy, files of flyers, and many suggestions to keep a project going. You can establish contact by dropping Gateway a note, with your name and address, asking for the free brochure, "Guide for Authors".

If you wish to deal with the book manufacturers directly it is time to write specifications so they can bid on the job. A number of them advertise in *The Genealogical Helper*, and quite a few will provide samples of their fine work. Most of this compiler's book have been printed and bound by BookCrafters, Inc., 140 Buchanan Street, P. O. Box 370, Chelsea, MI 48118.

If the need for a very small edition is anticipated you might wish to deal with The Anundsen Publishing Company, 108 Washington Street, Box 230, Decorah, Iowa 52101 [telephone (319) 382-4295]. If you contact them early enough they will provide, at small cost, instructions for preparing your materials for printing. Anundsen Publishing can print as few as one hundred copies at a reasonable price, their most economic size being eight and one-half by eleven inches, in which they specialize. Their custom half tones are excellent.

Of course there are a number of book manufacturers which will be glad to have your business: Academy Books, 10 Cleveland Avenue, P. O. Box 757, Rutland, VT 05702 [(802) 773-9194]; Adams Press, 25 East Washington Street, Chicago, IL 60602 [(708) 676-3426]; Braun-Brumfield, Inc., 100 North Staebler Road, P. O. Box 1203, Ann Arbor, MI 48106 [(313) 662-3291]; Cushing-Malloy, Inc., 1350 North Main Street, P. O. Box 8632, Ann Arbor, MI 48107 [(313) 663-8554, Fax (313) 663-5731], and Delmar Printing & Publishing, 6025 Metcalf Lane, Suite 2, Overland Park, MO 66202 [(800) 762-4861] are just some of the book manufacturers who work to the specifications of most genealogical publishers, including hard covers and small runs.

The list continues with Henington Publishing Company, 1 Main Street, Wolfe City, TX 75496 [(214) 496-2226)]; Inter-Collegiate Press, 6015 Travis Lane, P. O. Box 10, Shawnee Mission, KS 66201 [(913) 432-8100]; Jostens Printing and Publishing, 5501 Norman Center Drive, Minneapolis, MN 55437 [(612) 830-8415], with printing plants in Pennsylvania, Tennessee, Kansas and California, and Meriden-Stinehour, 47 Billard Street, P. O. Box 747, Meriden, CT 06450 [(203) 235-7929].

The list concludes with Quinn-Woodbine, Oceanview Road, P. O. Box 515, Woodbine, NJ 08270 [(609) 861-5352 or (212) 581-9288]; Rose Printing Company, Inc., P. O. Box 5708, Tallahassee, FL 32314 [(904) 576-4151 or (800) 227-3725]; Spilman Printing, 1801 Ninth Street, P. O.

Box 340218, Sacramento, CA 95834 [(916 or 800) 448-3511]; Thomson-Shore, Inc., 7300 West Joy Road, Dexter, MI 48130 [(313) 426-3939, Fax (313) 426-6219]; and Walsworth Publishing, 306 North Kansas Avenue, Marceline, MO 64658 [(816) 376-3543, Fax (816) 258-7798].

If you want a much more complete list, send a self-addressed stamped envelope to John Kremer, Ad-Lib Publications, P. O. Box 1102, Fairfield, IA 52556, and ask him to send you the latest ordering information of his *Directory of Short-Run Book Printers*, an excellent book providing many details and comments from customers of various firms, as well as ratings.

You must compare bids carefully, for shipping can be a major item of expense. Companies located closer to the source of paper will be cheaper, but those close to home may be easier to work with. Many of these firms will provide advice or pamphlets of instructions at small cost, but unless you feel you have the knowledge to handle all these details you may wish to deal with Gateway Press, which has remained a favorite with the readers of earlier editions of this book.

Any book manufacturer will need to know the quantity of copies desired, the trim size, number of pages (can be estimated, but is best a multiple of 16 or 32), what sort of copy will be provided, the stock or type of paper desired (book paper or acid free), the quality and color of the binding, including binder board, end sheets, bands and spine die, as well as the packing desired. In addition a request should be made for an estimate of shipping charges and the details of the terms of payment. If a publisher is requesting credit terms, a financial statement should be enclosed with the request for a bid. Kremer's book deals with a Request for Quotation form in detail.

It is most important to order an adequate supply of books. Many compilers do not order enough copies and then have to go to the expense of ordering a second printing at considerable cost if they do not wish to refuse many orders. Generally speaking, if you have completed a family history which includes a variety of surnames and you are confident of receiving at least one hundred pre-publication orders, it will be necessary to order at least five hundred copies, and perhaps seven hundred or more. Thus the letter requesting bids should state the minimum number which might be ordered and the need for a quotation of the price per each additional one hundred copies. It should be remembered that the very first copy is the expensive one, and all additional copies will each cost, most likely, only two to four dollars more; this price includes the cost of casebinding, or hard cover!

If you have compiled a family history of strictly limited interest, which has generated a pre-publication demand of not more than thirty copies, you should still have at least one hundred printed. The other seventy will be sold as a result of the listing with the Library of Congress and in *Books in Print* (about which you will be given the details by R.R. Bowker when they respond to your request for an International Standard Book Number), and minimal display advertising, although it may take several years for the edition to be sold.

The trim size of the book refers to the size of an individual page, without the binding. This book is six inches by nine inches. A slightly smaller size, which is quite popular, is five and one-half inches by eight and one-half inches. The smaller size is about nine per cent cheaper to produce. Doubling the size of the page nearly doubles the cost of the book.

In considering the number of pages of the book, keep in mind that usually you pay for the number of signatures, or groups of pages which must be printed on a large press, rather than the actual number of pages. It is cheaper to have a number divided by 32, or perhaps 16, than to have an odd number of pages requiring a signature to be hand processed and cut. Of course some of the pages in front and back can be blank.

If all the copy to be submitted for publication consists of typed and typeset copy, and line drawings, the manufacturer can prepare the plates for printing in one step. If photographs or other pictures are to be included it will be more complicated, and hence more expensive. The best way to include good quality photographs is to submit glossy prints of the size to be printed, trimmed exactly as they should appear, so that half-tones can be made by the book manufacturer. Half tones are the master copies in which the photo has been reproduced in the form of dots in the fashion used in newspapers. They can be printed as part of a normal page, and can be of very high quality. The manufacturer should be consulted concerning the cost of any other process, such as the inclusion of plates of pictures in the book, which will be more expensive but perhaps well worth the cost.

The manufacturer will provide samples upon request of the paper and cover stocks available. You might wish to know how many sheets of paper comprise a book an inch thick, for example, to assist in preparation of the copy for the spine die in terms of size. Most of this publisher's books have been printed on normal sixty pound book paper, which is thick enough that the print does not show through the page too readily but is reasonable in price. Book paper, however, is not acid-free, and will deteriorate in time. You might wish to specify acid free paper as a result, or at least request information as to the difference in cost.

This volume is bound in Type C Roxite with head bands. Type C has proven to be much stronger than type B, which was used in the production of the original edition of *Ancestral Lines*. The head bands are the decorative strips you can see as you look at the end of the book (top or bottom) at the end of the pages next to the binding. They add a touch of quality at little cost.

The binder boards are the sheets of cardboard inside the cloth of the hard cover, and here are .088 inches thick, and have proven to be adequate. The end sheets, the paper glued to the inside of the covers and forming the blank page between the front cover and the title page, must be heavier than the book paper used. The manufacturer's recommendation should be requested. Plain white end sheets will be adequate unless you wish to imitate an older style of binding.

The die(s) for stamping the cloth cover will be made, probably, by a subcontractor. It is a metal stamp using the camera-ready copy you have submitted for the spine and perhaps the front cover. The type used for the cover die(s) should be relatively large and open, so that the stamping will be clear. The cost of the die(s) is not great (perhaps $20 to $50), and may be omitted from the manufacturer's quotation since he does not directly control this cost.

The packaging should be considered with care. The books will probably be shipped to you by truck, with many boxes packed on a skid. The movement of the books within the boxes during shipping may cause wear on the bindings, so shrink wrapping the books may be considered necessary to prevent this form of damage. In addition, if you order the books to be shrink wrapped individually, they will be protected that much more when mailed in Jiffy bags, so this is probably worth the extra cost of about ten cents per book, except perhaps for the number of copies needed to fill prepublication orders, which are going to be autographed prior to mailing.

When the books are being prepared for mailing it is a simple matter to slit the wrap slightly at the top, slip an invoice or receipt with another flyer between the shrink wrap and the cover of the book, and then put it in a Jiffy bag. As long as the invoice and book flyer are the only enclosures the package can be sent book rate as long as it is stamped (with a rubber stamp which can be ordered at a local printshop or stationery store) which reads, "BOOKS Special Fourth Class Rate." Even if the packing falls apart in the mails, the invoice, if inserted so the addressee can be noted through the shrink wrap, will assure delivery by the Postal Service. Should you get a large order, do not mail a full box of books in the original carton without reenforcing it liberally with filament tape, particularly at the corner where the carton was glued together as well as along previously taped seams.

Returning to the question of bids, some book manufacturers are very quick to respond to requests for bids or quotations while others are slow to do so. The bidding process should be given plenty of time, as the slowest bidder may be considerably cheaper than the rest. Once bids have been received you can narrow your list to a few companies with whom you will discuss terms in greater detail, and perhaps handle the questions concerning the handling of photographs and the providing of samples. Of course you will have to keep in mind that bids are good only for a limited time, and you may wish to request a fresh quote immediately prior to sending the copy for manufacturing. Further, it is helpful to know the manufacturer cannot control the precise number of books printed, so there will always be a few "overs", for which you will pay the minimal cost pro rated according to the cost of an additional hundred copies.

You must be aware that the bids will vary considerably. Following are bids received on this book in early 1990, including freight:

1500 copies	2000 copies
$3,172 including dies	$3,881
$3,860	$4,910
$3,871	$4,380
$4,062	$5,009
$4,630	$5,815
$5,569	$6,891
$6,081	$7,339
$7,249	$9,265
$7,839	$9,624

Once you have come to terms you will have to send, perhaps by registered mail, the complete camera-ready copy including the typewritten text, the typeset title and copyright pages, and the copy for the die(s) used to stamp the spine (and perhaps the front cover). If the final number of pages is not the same as specified in the bid, the price could change, but may not as long as they do not require an extra signature, or special handling of a planned signature.

The copy must be accompanied by specific instructions in writing, particularly concerning the amount of reduction, if any, and the number of copies to be printed and bound, with reference to the quotation. Provide your phone number and the hours during working days when you can be reached, keeping in mind any time zone differences. Hopefully by the time it is necessary to deal with last minute questions over the phone you will be able to discuss them intelligently without seeing more samples.

You can begin advertising the pre-publication sale as soon as you have an estimate of the cost of publication, including binding and shipping. If you believe that one hundred orders will be received prior to your sending the copy to the book manufacturer, the price can be determined by dividing the quotation or bid by one hundred. The immediate objective should be to recover the manufacturing cost in advance, with the costs of copy preparation, research, the advertising campaign and the like to be recovered from later sales.

Hopefully, the pre-publication flyers will go into the mail at least one month before the copy will be ready for the manufacturer. This will allow orders to come in so financial demands can be met as they arise, without adding interest to the costs of production. The flyer should state the title of the book, the compiler's name, the scope and features of the volume, the approximate number of pages, type of binding and the pre-publication price, stating clearly that this is a discounted price which will expire by a specific date by which all orders must be postmarked. Perhaps three hundred flyers will generate one hundred orders, but the flyers should be mailed only to those who have known the work has been in progress, not to the general public. The flyers can be printed from typed copy, or can employ duplicate copy of the typesetting, cut and pasted with typewritten copy. If this has been planned the duplicate copies of the typesetting should have been ordered from the printer at the same time the originals were ordered.

The preparation of flyers for general circulation should wait until the book has been finished and readied for mailing to the manufacturer, if for no other reason than the fact that you will want to be able to advertise the specific number of pages. Be sure that the ad copy has been written and checked for all needed information before you put the camera-ready copy into the mail. Have you checked it for the number of pages, for the Library of Congress Catalog Card Number and the International Standard Book Number? The scope of the book might well be restated, stressing the families included without dwelling upon the fact that the volume deals specifically with one's ancestry.

The flyer must be very neat and free of errors, as recipients will assume the book has been compiled with the same care. The size of the flyer will be determined by the amount of advertising copy on it, but the layout should be done with the method of mailing in mind. Pre-publication flyers might be more effective if mailed in envelopes which have been hand addressed. If mailing labels have been prepared they can be saved for the mailing of a second flyer, after publication, to those who did not order in time to take advantage of the discount. Of course the labels for those who did order can be applied to Jiffy bags as orders come in, so that you are ready for the mailing on publication day. Remember that first class mail, hand addressed, will not only be forwarded as necessary, but is more likely to be opened and read.

However, the cost of envelopes can be saved if the folded flyer meets Postal Service regulations. An eight and one-half by eleven sheet folded tightly in thirds will do, as will an eight and one-half by fourteen sheet folded in fourths to a size of eight and one-half by three and one-half. However, three and one-half inches is the minimum height acceptable, so do not use a thirteen inch sheet folded in fourths unless you are willing to mail all the flyers in envelopes. All flyers mailed outside the country must be in envelopes, sealed, and should be sent by air.

The layout of any flyer must be planned with care, even though the following instructions pertain primarily to those intended to be sent without envelopes. On the first side, which may be the only printed side, the ad copy should occupy all but the bottom fold (perhaps three and one-half inches from the fold to the bottom of the sheet), which should be reserved for use as an order form. Once the flyers have been printed the other side of the order form should be used to address the piece. Thus, when the order form has been returned you will know to whom the piece was addressed originally. Once the flyer has been printed and folded, the return address, if not printed on the reverse of the original piece, can be applied with a rubber stamp ordered at the stationery store or at the printer who did the flyers.

While it is not possible to illustrate an actual flyer in a book of this size without making the illustration so small as to be almost illegible, the text of the pre-publication flyer might be similar to the following example.

Pre-publication Announcement

ANCESTRAL LINES REVISED

190 Families in England, Wales, Germany,
New England, New York, New Jersey and Pennsylvania.

Casebound, fully indexed by personal names, places and ships will full bibliography and citations to sources, about 650 pages. ISBN 0-936124-0-5-9.

Some of the lineages in this volume include the families of: Abell, Allen, Allsop, Althouse, Anthony, Babcock, Battin, Bennett, Bliss, Borden, Borton, Bosworth, Bowen, Bowne, Boyer, Brown, Brownell, Bullock, Campbell, Carpenter, Chase, Cheyney, Coggeshall, Debozear, Dodge, Evans, Fowler, Freeborn, Frost, George, Griesemer, Hathaway, Hazard,

Howland, Hull, Hunt, Jefferis, Kent, Kirby, Kruse, Lawton, Ludwig, Marshall, Matlack, Paine, Peabody, Perry, Potter, Read, Remington, Slade, Smedley, Talbot, Taylor, Tefft, Tilley, Tripp, Vandenburgh, Visscher, White and Wodell.

In addition, 129 other families are treated, comprising all those about which this compiler has corresponded with genealogists in the past ten years. The families are presented in alphabetical order to permit this work to be used with ease as a reference.

This volume is a completely revised and extensively rewritten edition combining materials from the first edition of *Ancestral Lines* and *Slade-Babcock Genealogy*, with some corrections and extensive additions resulting from continuing research and correspondence.

Those who are familiar with the earlier works may wish to consider purchasing this revised edition at the special pre-publication price of $42.00 postpaid (California residents only add local sales tax). Not only have families been brought up to date to include new addresses and vital statistics, as well as additional biographical detail, but the ancestry has been more fully developed.

Orders must be postmarked by November 15th in order to receive the volume at the pre-publication price, which is discounted substantially from retail. However, upon request your check will be held for another thirty days before it is cashed.

Please understand that the volume is scheduled to be sent to the book manufacturer on November 16th, and publication will take place in January or February.

If you would like your copy to be autographed by the compiler, please indicate this on your order form. Your copy can be inscribed to you personally, numbered, dated the day of publication, and autographed.

Please return the order form below with your check or money order to the compiler: Carl Boyer, 3rd, P. O. Box 333, Santa Clarita, CA 91322.

To: Carl Boyer, 3rd   From: _____
    P. O. Box 333   _____
    Santa Clarita, CA 91322   _____

Please send me upon publication ___ copy or copies of *Ancestral Lines Revised: 190 Families in England, Wales, Germany, New England, New York, New Jersey and Pennsylvania.* I enclose the special pre-publication price of $42.00 postpaid per copy (with sales tax to be added only by California residents). I enclose my check or money order for $_____.

___Please inscribe my copy personally to _____
___Please autograph, date and number my copy without an inscription.

Having placed the flyers into the mails you have really gone into business. It becomes increasingly important, at this point, to keep the deadline which you have promised, and this can be difficult if you have not allowed much time for the completion of remaining work on the master copy, for after ten days or so orders will be coming in and needing processing, adding to your chores.

Furthermore it has become time to check on the need for meeting state requirements concerning the collection and reporting of sales taxes. The printer who has done the flyers is a good source of information concerning the address of the state agency you must contact. It may be wise to call your city or county clerk to find out whether you should have a business license. The paperwork is minimal. Small publishers are under no obligation to collect sales taxes from out-of-state customers.

Invoices can be purchased from a stationery store and stamped with your name and address. A ledger book will help in the keeping of the necessary records for the state and federal tax people. As orders are received the invoices (marked paid) should be made out and kept in order, with the names for personal inscriptions noted on them with care. Jiffy bags should be purchased in lots of one hundred, at which point the unit price is less than half the cost of a single bag. The bags should be addressed as orders are received, and piled up in order to await the day of publication.

Once the books arrive from the manufacturer, publication should take place promptly. By legal definition, publication occurs the day that the books are first offered for sale and immediate delivery, or are distributed. The first three copies pulled out of the first opened box (if not already snatched by members of your own family) should be set aside for the Library of Congress. Form TX must be filled out and sent off with the copyright fee ($10. at this writing) and two copies of the book, while the third copy must go to the Cataloging in Publication program. However, the Form TX can be dated a few days away, the date you anticipate all pre-publication orders will be filled. Thus you will have the time, without staying up all night, to autograph and date and pack the books going out in the first mailing.

Books mailed to addresses in the United States can be sent either book rate or library rate, depending on the recipient. All books mailed to or from libraries or institutions of learning qualify for the library rate and should be labeled "Book-Library Rate" rather than stamped for the special fourth class rate. The library rate is a little more than half the normal book rate. Prior to the actual mailing on publication day a copy of the packaged book should be taken to the post office for weighing, and enough stamps purchased so they can be affixed at leisure.

It can be quite thrilling publishing that first book, and, recognizing that many are anxious to have their copies as soon as possible, you may wish to stay up all night getting the mailing chores done. However, be careful while you are doing the autographing, not only to spell the names on the inscriptions with care but to be sure that all the books are right side up and turned in the proper direction.

You will be busy during the weeks following the mailing of the copy to the manufacturer with jobs other than preparing the pre-publication orders. You will have to write copy for flyers to go to reviewers, dealers, newspaper columnists and the general public. While the latter flyers may be printed from typed copy, it is worthwhile to spend a little extra to have typesetting done, providing that you work closely with the printer on the format and style, and proofread the results carefully before ordering the printing and folding of thousands of pieces.

Once your manufacturer has sent you confirmation of their shipping date these flyers should go into the mail. The text will be considerably different from that of the pre-publication offer, and the price should reflect a healthy increase, for at this point you must remember that the task is to recover the cost of the preparation of the camera-ready copy (including the expense for the typewriter or a portion of that new computer), the costs of advertising and mailing, and the need to make a profit to be reported for tax purposes, as the Internal Revenue Service will not allow deductions for business expenses unless you can indeed report a profit within five years of beginning the business.

If you have purchased a copy of Anita Cheek Milner's *Newspaper Genealogical Column Directory* from Heritage Books, and have made a list of other reviewers mentioned in *The Genealogical Helper*, and made up a number of addressed envelopes as a result, it will be relatively simple to put out a mailing with the idea of obtaining maximum exposure through book reviews. Each reviewer should be sent a press release, which may be photocopied and which most will discard, and an order form for a complimentary review copy of your book. While reviewers will often review a book which has been sent unsolicited, the review is more likely to appear under the by-lines of those who have requested a copy. Some will simply print the press release rather than take the time to do the review, however, so some effort should go into making it appear professionally written.

Good newspaper copy gets right to the point: who, what, when, where, why and how. Paragraphs are short, and the entire release should be one page or less, doublespaced with one inch margins. Again, avoid describing the work as being about one's own ancestry and stress its usefulness as a reference.

Following is the text of a sample release:

For further information: Carl Boyer, 3rd
                          P. O. Box 333
                          Santa Clarita, CA 91322
                          (805) 259-3154 after 4:00 p.m. Pacific Time
For immediate release.

ANCESTRAL LINES TELLS STORY OF 190 FAMILIES

Carl Boyer, 3rd, compiler of three previous family histories and four volumes of Ship Passenger Lists, has now published his latest work, Ancestral Lines Revised, which tells the story in a form suitable for reference of 190 families with roots in Europe, New England and the Middle Atlantic region.

In one 666-page volume Boyer has woven the documented histories of families coming to America from England, Wales and Germany, settling in Plymouth Colony, Massachusetts Bay, Rhode Island, New York, New Jersey and Pennsylvania, and spreading their descendants among forty-nine states and many foreign countries.

The families include Abell, Allen, Anthony, Babcock, Bliss, Borden, Bosworth, Bowen, Bowne, Boyer, Brown, Campbell, Carpenter, Chase, Coggeshall, Dodge, Frost, George, Hathaway, Hazard, Howland, Kirby, Lawton, Ludwig, Paine, Read, Remington, Slade, Tilley, Vanderbilt, White and many others, with a number of them traced to their European origins dating back over 500 years.

Treated alphabetically, each line is fully documented, and complete name and place indexes assist the reader who is searching for some of his own ancestors.

Boyer explained, "I have been working on this project for twenty years in my spare time and have included the ancestry of hundreds of living Americans. Indeed, there are millions more unnamed who are descendants of the early generations of the families about whom this book was done."

Boyer, who is a social studies teacher at San Fernando High School in Los Angeles and Mayor of the City of Santa Clarita, has been listed in Who's Who in Genealogy and Heraldry.

A flyer listing all the family names treated in the book is available to all those mailing Boyer a self-addressed stamped envelope. Write to Carl Boyer, 3rd, P. O. Box 333, Santa Clarita, CA 91322.

The book is available for immediate delivery at $48.00 postpaid.

An analysis of the above release may be of some use. The first two paragraphs contain the essential ingredients of a news story and hopefully spark some interest on the part of the reader. The third lists some names (never enough) and implies that the book is a quality work. The next, a quotation, makes Boyer seem to be a real person and contains a sales pitch as well. The fifth lists credentials. The next offers a way of obtaining more information and the last offers the book.

No, press releases do not sell many books. Nor do reviews, generally, the exceptions being those with truly commercial titles, such as *Ship Passenger Lists: the South (1538-1825)* or *How to Publish and Market Your Family History*. But they do help the publisher gain recognition, and some readers will suggest the purchase of the book to a local genealogical or historical society.

The press release should be accompanied by a letter explaining that copies of the book are available for review purposes free of charge, and that the publisher would appreciate being sent a copy of any mention of his work. The letter could be printed with a request form at the bottom, to be returned by the reviewer wanting a free copy. All review copies should be mailed with an advertising flyer enclosed so the reviewer will know the price and ordering information.

If sales warrant the mailing of additional flyers after the first batch have gone into the mail it may be helpful to plan a flyer with revised copy, including quotations from reviews. Genealogists generally fail to do this, perhaps because of a feeling that it smacks of commercialism, but good quotes, not taken out of context, can be helpful.

Flyers printed from typeset copy should be available by the thousands. Letters to dealers known from the pages of *The Genealogical Helper* may result in sales if sent with a copy of the flyer and if they mention terms. Typically, dealers, wholesalers and jobbers may expect a forty per cent discount from list, to which price should be added the cost of postage and handling (the stamps and the Jiffy bag or box). "Net 30 days" can be typed into the terms space on the invoice. Many will not pay in thirty days, but would take a discount for prompt payment if it is offered, even when they are late. Dealers generally do pay with reasonable speed. Wholesalers, jobbers and libraries can be slower, to the point that this publisher now insists on payment in advance.

The first mailing of flyers intended for general circulation should go to libraries, genealogical societies and individuals who have indicated an interest in certain families in genealogical periodicals. Perhaps 3,000 flyers will be needed, and the costs of typesetting, printing and mailing first class may be more than $1,000. You must be prepared to wait for months, and perhaps years in the case of a few orders, for the returns from these flyers. Libraries are slow to react. Genealogical societies have limited book budgets and will order as funds become available. In the case of mailings to dealers, one need only write "Wholesale to Dealers" on the face of the flyer to get their interest, but they may not order, if at all, until they have seen reviews or review quotes.

The request for an International Standard Book Number from R.R. Bowker will have resulted in their asking for data on the book to be published, with the result that your work will be listed in *Books in Print* and in the Bowker computer data bank. These reference tools are used by librarians and book dealers for ordering, as are the new listings from the Library of Congress. Jobbers ordering for libraries will make contact. Libraries, dealers and jobbers will generally want to be invoiced in triplicate, should be given credit, and are often slow to pay. One must be patient, but after 120 days a reminder will help.

Family histories should also be listed in *Genealogical & Local History Books in Print*. If you do not have a copy of this resource, recommended above, information concerning a paid listing may be requested from Genealogical Books in Print, 6818 Lois Drive, Springfield, VA 22150. This work is an effective selling tool which will generate orders for years, but as it appears infrequently you must meet the deadlines.

It may prove worthwhile, depending on the nature of the book being sold, to offer genealogical societies an opportunity to allow their members to order directly from them, allowing the society to send the publisher a list of customers to whom copies can be mailed directly. Under these circumstances the society might be expected to pay the wholesale price (a 40% discount from retail), plus mailing costs, the same terms given to dealers. It frequently costs 40% of the retail price to advertise, so such an arrangement is rewarding, particularly if the number of flyers to be mailed directly is minimal due to the limited scope of a work.

During the period in which you were researching and compiling material for the family history you became aware of a number of appropriate journals in which display ads might be placed. A form letter to each of these periodicals asking for information on the placement of ads should be mailed at least six months prior to the anticipated date of publication. Once you have received replies it will be time to evaluate each journal to determine whether or not a display ad may prove to be worthwhile.

Many journals circulate to a few hundred, or at most a little more than one thousand, readers and libraries. Only *The Genealogical Helper* can be said to reach a "mass" audience, with a circulation of more than 45,000. An effort should be made to consider advertising costs on the basis of the number of readers. However, you should also plan to advertise in periodicals which may be targeted to appropriate potential customers even if the cost per thousand readers is considerably higher. Display ads are much more cost effective than direct mail, even if direct mail will sell more books in the long run.

Having all the information on display advertising at hand several months before publication will permit you to have camera-ready copy typeset by the local printer in the size to be used most commonly. This copy can be sent to all journals either for use as is or as a sample of the way the ad should appear. If a particular periodical does not sell space to fit the ad a larger space can be purchased. White space is very effective in attracting attention.

It is very helpful to know the source of each order. Therefore, the camera-ready copy should include a small blank space within the publisher's address. Right after the publisher's name should be a line reading "Dept." Before each ad is sent to a periodical you should type a unique department number or code directly on the copy. Readers responding to this publisher at Dept. GH-5 are generally not aware that by addressing their orders in this way they are not only advising the publisher that they saw the ad in a particular issue of *The Genealogical Helper*, but that they are also supporting that periodical by encouraging more advertising in that medium in the future.

As has been mentioned, display advertising is generally much more cost effective than direct mail, but will generate fewer orders than mailed flyers. That is to say that an ad in *The Genealogical Helper* costing $78 may generate $500 worth of orders, and it may take 500 flyers costing $180 for printing and postage (not including any compensation for the work of addressing them) to generate another $500 in orders. Display ads and direct mail work hand in hand, reinforcing each other. This publisher has received many orders addressed to a department number advertised in a magazine but including an order form from the direct mail piece.

The number of flyers to be mailed will vary considerably with the nature of the work being offered. It is necessary to target the mailings carefully, sending them only to those customers most likely to be interested in a particular work, if you have only one title for sale. This publisher mailed 30,000 flyers in 1980, when a first class stamp cost fifteen cents, and managed to receive a return of a little less than one dollar for each piece mailed. Each mailing piece cost about thirty cents, including the printing of the flyers, postage and paying for the addressing of labels, which was done by hand, so the return did not only cover the cost of each piece, but the cost of inventory and some profit. However, in 1980 this publisher was advertising five titles, including the four volumes of *Ship Passenger Lists*, so it was likely that at least one title would have some appeal to any genealogist receiving the flyer.

Unless you have a computer to generate mailing labels it is not very practical to try to avoid duplicate mailings to the same address. Good lists are collected by noting those who placed queries in various periodicals, and from directories listing the surname interests of members of various societies. Some duplication of mailings is helpful, for a second mailing will generate more orders. If you consistently try to be alert so you will not send more than two pieces to any one address, you will find, after a period of months, that your memory is developing to the point that it is possible to recall whether a specific address is likely to be a duplicate.

While it is quite obvious to any publisher that customers will recognize displays and flyers as advertising, public reaction to press releases and reviews is curious. Many seem to believe that reviews are ads, but press releases will also be interpreted as reviews. Do not hesitate to quote reviews in flyers, but a quotation taken out of context of the general tone of a review will damage your reputation not only with customers but also the reviewers, who are sensitive about their own reputations.

Once you have received the books from the manufacturer it is time to mail your press release. Some genealogical columnists will ignore it, others will simply note the availability of your work, with ordering information from the release, while others, who have not responded to receipt of the flyer advising that review copies are available, will be jogged by the release to request a complimentary copy. If a reviewer does ask for a copy it should be sent with the flyer so the ordering information can be made part of the review. Also, enclose a note requesting a copy of the review itself. A review copy will frequently result in the book being given the major part of a weekly column in a general circulation newspaper, or perhaps a whole chain of newspapers.

Some reviews will not result in orders while others will elicit a very good return. Relatively few large papers print genealogy columns, but a small weekly may well generate an order or two.

A major problem faced by a columnist writing a review of a family history is that of boiling the evaluation and a description of the contents into a few hundred words, or much less, as this publisher discovered when reviews of *Ancestral Lines Revised* appeared. One reviewer had telephoned to say that she could not describe the book within the length of her column, that listing the surnames alone was too much. The resulting conversation ended in agreement that her readers would be sent a descriptive flyer upon request, if they submitted a self-addressed, stamp envelope. Over fifty requests for flyers were received, but no orders for the book followed. However, one potential customer did buy a complete set of *Ship Passenger Lists*. Thus the compiler of a family history may wish to attempt to describe the contents of his book in thirty words or less, provide the information to the reviewer for optional use, and leave the evaluation of these contents for the reviewer alone to write.

Reviews may be good, bad, or mixed. One review of a work published in 1979 contained the admonition: "In-as-much as this book was published as recently as 1979 and medieval ancestries have appeared in certain genealogies much earlier,... an examination of more recent articles pertaining to these lineages appearing in periodicals such as The American Genealogist, the National Genealogical Society Quarterly, The New England Historical and Genealogical Register, and The Genealogist, would have been a useful form of preparation...." A comment such as this does make the customer pause, while a rave review will promote sales to people who simply enjoy reading good work, and perhaps have no personal interest in the families covered.

Finally it should be remembered that the preface and the copyright page are selling tools. The publisher's name and address should be printed at the bottom of the copyright page so that library users can write for ordering information. The address should also be typed at the end of the preface, which itself must be written with great care as it may be the only section of the book in which the author can demonstrate clearly his individual style of writing.

BUSINESS ASPECTS OF PUBLISHING

The genealogical publisher is not particularly likely to be both a businessman and a tax expert, and this writer truly does not fall into either category in spite of years of experience in the one-man publishing field. However, with the caveat that accounting may have to be left to accountants, some points concerning business practices and record keeping for tax purposes are presented here with the idea that the reader is more interested in preserving a reputation for integrity than becoming a "sharp" businessman.

As has been stated previously, the one thing a publisher must have is an address. This address must be stable, as orders generated by just one advertisement will be received over a period of years. However, an address and some good reviews (which, once they have appeared, can be quoted in display ads and on flyers) will not make a publisher successful. Publishing takes a lot of hard work with constant attention to scanning queries, working on ad copy, and getting flyers into the mail.

If you have had no experience as an independent businessperson, it may be a little nervewracking to contemplate going into business, keeping the necessary records, and complying with all of the appropriate laws and regulations. However, the genealogical publisher will generally find that the volume of business is so small that no great difficulties arise. As has already been suggested, your local printer can advise whether you need a permit to collect sales taxes, and provide the address to which you must write for information.

If you avoid both employing help and incorporating, paperwork will be kept to a minimum. In many states a person selling by mail order need not even buy a business license. All this publisher, a resident of the new city of Santa Clarita (population over 110,000) has had to do has been to pay one visit to the offices of the State Board of Equalization to obtain a seller's permit, file a sales tax return annually (a form which takes about fifteen minutes to complete if one has kept good books) and send a check for the collected taxes to the state, as well as file a Form C with both federal and state personal income tax returns.

When extra help has been needed, piece work was at first given to the publisher's children. As they left the nest the work was done on computer. A record of the work done, the rate and amount of payment, to whom payment was made with the record of the person's social security number, was kept. If substantial payments are involved a call to the Internal Revenue Service will provide the needed forms for reporting these payments so the recipients can be taxed. If those doing the piecework do not earn enough to be liable for federal or state income taxes, or social security payments as a self-employed person, these reports need not be filed. However, the payments must be itemized carefully on Form C.

It should be remembered that it is not government policy at any level to "hassle" people who make a sincere attempt to do the right thing. This publisher sold books for several years without collecting sales taxes, believing that it was not necessary when only a few books per year were sold within the state. His registration with the California State Board of Equalization occurred as a result of a library remitting the invoiced amount plus six per cent in sales tax. In an attempt to follow through, the amount involved (less than two dollars) was forwarded by check to the Franchise Tax Board, which collects state income taxes in California, with a cover letter. The check and letter were forwarded to the proper agency, which requested a conference.

The conference was not an unpleasant affair. The problem was reviewed thoroughly, the agent was satisfied there was no intent to avoid paying taxes, and the publisher was asked to pay only those taxes due for the preceding three years, with negligible penalty and interest, and the small amount due (about $17) was paid. Even in 1980, when gross sales exceeded $32,000, the sales tax return required payment of only about $187, and by that time taxes were being collected and returns filed regularly.

It will be necessary for the publisher to keep track of inventory. The book manufacturer's records of the number of copies shipped and billed will be accessible to the tax collection agencies. Each book sold should be recorded on an invoice slip. Invoices for individuals paying at the time of the order should be in duplicate, with the second copy kept by the seller. Invoices to institutions being billed on a credit basis must be prepared in quadruplicate, as many of these institutions want three copies, the second one having been kept by the publisher.

Invoices should be recorded in the ledger book as they are paid, with the copy for the files marked with the date payment was received so any auditor can check against the ledger and bank deposit records. Ledgers should be kept current so that negative cash flow can be kept to a minimum. No loss can be reported the fifth year a business is in operation without grave risk of having previous business losses taken as deductions thrown out by the tax people on the basis that the "business" is really a hobby. The ledger book must show all the information which is needed to complete income and sales tax returns, with one section for expenses and one for receipts.

The income section should contain pages with columns headed: date, payer, state of residence, payment for book, payment for postage, payment for sales tax (which a small business collects only from residents of the same state), out-of-state retail sales, wholesale, in-state retail sales, and gross receipts. It may be necessary to separate sales tax records according to whether they are within one's own county or not. The figure in the payment for book column should be duplicated in either the out-of-state retail sales, wholesale, or in-state retail sales column (to expedite completion of the sales tax return as well as reconciling the accuracy of each page of records), and each page must be balanced as it is completed. Each column must be added (carrying forward any figures from the previous page). The total of the payments for books column plus those for postage and sales taxes must then equal the total of gross receipts. Then the payments for postage and taxes should be added to the out-of-state, wholesale, and in-state sales to again equal gross receipts. A public accountant, or perhaps a friend with small business experience, can assist with setting up a simple system for the ledger.

It is also wise to mark on the invoice and the ledger book a notation of the source of sale, if known. That is, if the customer mentions having read a review, or encloses an order form from a flyer, or addresses the order to a department number, this should be noted. Keep good records of review copies sent, flyers mailed (by date and style), and display ads placed. Perhaps you will find that some forms of advertising are providing a fair return but others are not.

Business expenses are recorded in a separate section of the ledger book, with columns headed: date, payee, check or receipt number, postage, ad printing, ad fees or space, office supplies, research fees, dues and subscriptions, inventory printing and purchase, utilities, miscellaneous, perhaps a category for contract piece work or leases, and the annual running total.

The keeping of accurate records in an up-to-date fashion will enable you to know whether income is exceeding expenses. Once one is in danger of losing money it is time to suspend operations. The books remaining in inventory will sell eventually. Word of mouth is powerful, and the continuing expense of ads should not be borne if it results in negative cash flow.

Of course the ledger book must have been established at the outset of going into the genealogical publishing business. However, no business losses can be taken on Form C until you are confident of being able to report a profit within five years. Since a typewriter or computer can be written off as a business expense, this cost can be reported over the years from the time it was acquired until it has been written off. Here you might wish to consult a tax accountant. Tax law does change from year to year.

Genealogical publishing is a terrible business. Readers of this book should be able to accomplish the specific goal of publishing and marketing a family history at no personal loss, and perhaps some taxable profit. Certainly every effort should be made to develop eventual taxable profits which will exceed early losses so that your intent as a business person cannot be challenged. However, a genealogical publisher will not find much help.

Good mailing lists are not readily available, although this writer has developed the capability of printing a list of more than 30,000 active genealogists on labels, as well as over 2,000 genealogical libraries, and is willing to provide them for limited purposes at standard rates. While direct mail will generally increase sales over a campaign limited to display ads, it is much more expensive and for some publications cannot be cost effective.

The market is limited, if growing. Only a handful of businesses in the field have been successful over a number of years. This is why the smartest thing a family historian can do is to publish the book, make the profit and quit the business before the positive cash flow stops. The inventory will have been paid for. Receipts may have been adequate to pay the other costs as well. You will have done your duty as a taxpayer, and above all you will have the satisfaction of knowing that the family history has been done.

If, after a few years, some inventory still remains, perhaps additional advertising will be in order, but such ads should specifically mention the limited number of copies available and should probably reflect a price increase, perhaps a substantial one. Books should not be discounted as remainders if you might ever publish again, in order to discourage people from waiting to order at a discount. Hopefully all books will be sold before inflation increases the costs of advertising and mailing too much.

However, you are warned that finishing a book is like losing a member of the family. It is worse if the reviews have been good and customers write of their appreciation. There is always the temptation, then, to do something more. That is why the *Ship Passenger Lists* series was done, why *Ancestral Lines Revised* was published, and why this book was written. Once you have finished the family history you may feel that you have more to offer, that the needs of genealogists in general might be met by the publication of just one more title.

The four volumes of *Ship Passenger Lists* were conceived because of frustration at the massive effort needed to survey the periodical literature each time the question of the origins of an immigrant ancestor was considered. For three years this publisher waited patiently for someone else to do the job, before finally deciding to put a year's spare time into preparing the first volume. A few pre-publication orders were solicited, and the copy was sent to the book manufacturer. What happened just days before the books were delivered? Yes! Genealogical Publishing came out with a new title which duplicated half the material in this compiler's work. As it turned out, sales of both titles were strong enough to encourage the continue of the series by both publishers, but imagine the feeling of devastation at the time that flyer was received!

Many one-time publishers are intellectuals who may or may not like the world of publishing. Frankly, the tedium of ad campaigns, the typing of thousands of addresses into computer files, and the constant scanning of queries for potential customers can be good therapy, helping you to forget the ailments of the world. If you like the business you will continue to find opportunities. These will make themselves manifest as earlier projects have been developing. How many people who have published just one book would like to have a distributor to promote it within the special world of genealogists?

THE REVISION

Once the manufactured copies of the book have been delivered and the pre-publication orders have been filled, the ad campaign has been set and the first batch of flyers has gone into the mail, you must pause to think about what is going to happen to your work. Reviewers may suggest improvements, correspondents will cite errors (which are always present) and contribute new data, relatives will arise from their slumbers and finally submit long sought information, and new publications will suggest other additions to what has been written and set forth in black and white. Thus the planning of a revised edition is imperative.

This is not to suggest that the revised edition must be issued within a specified time. If you will recall something stated earlier in this work, the worst thing a small publisher can do is to print too few copies of a book. It may take years to sell all of the stock on hand, particularly if cash flow indicates that renewed advertising will not result in the original relatively high level of orders. While it is true that the turnover among family history enthusiasts is high, and it does take a long time to make the genealogical world conscious of one's title, constant advertising of the same title will bring steadily diminishing returns. Indeed, a major reason (aside from continuing dealer demand) this compiler's series of *Ship Passenger Lists* went into reprintings is that new titles have borne the advertising costs. Once a title has gone out of print the level of continuing orders is not usually high enough to merit reprints being done.

However, if you take steps immediately upon publication to prepare for the eventual printing of a revised edition, the second volume may well became a reality. As the years pass the younger members of the family will want their own copies of the genealogy, and will be delighted to learn that an updated, revised edition, rather than simply a reprint, will be available.

Once the camera-ready copy has gone to the manufacturer you may experience a feeling of being in limbo, so to speak, unless you have made a photocopy of the work (or have it on computer disk). Once the books are in hand you should set one aside as a working copy, so that marginal notes and references to files can be made as new materials are gathered and the reviews appear. You should also establish a new drafts file. If your copy was typewritten, rather than produced on a computer printer, it should be put in a safe place and clearly labeled so that anyone could understand its value. If the type for the original copy was chosen carefully you may find that some, perhaps many, of the original pages can be reused, perhaps only with changes to the headings and page numbers. In the case of *Ancestral Lines* this compiler did not like the way the original typeface appeared in reduced printing (it was a little light), and so the revised edition was completely retyped. This led to much more rewriting than might have otherwise been the case. Of course it was not appreciated at the time how simple preparing a new edition can be once the original has been saved on computer disks.

The nice thing about working on a revision is that it might be done with relatively little effort, unless, of course, you continue to research unresolved problems with vigor. As new materials appear in print they should be noted in the working copy and the bibliography. Key relatives will hopefully maintain contact and continue to provide new materials. It would be wise to send out a form letter annually to these people asking if there are any address changes or vital statistics to be recorded. Many computer word processing programs contain a mailing list feature which will help address envelopes or postcards quickly, which makes a mailing requesting information a simple job. Just stamp "Address Correction Requested" under your return address on the face of the mailing if you want the post office to notify you of any changes, at fees equivalent to a first class stamp or a little more per item. If the annual mailing goes out in early September it will get you the maximum return from the post office records of address changes, which are often purged in October.

Depending on whether the first edition has been sold out within a couple of years or has lingered in stock for five or ten, and considering how often orders keep coming in even though advertising has been discontinued for some time, you may decide to begin the production of new camera-ready copy on the day the first edition has sold out, or delay that task for months or years, or perhaps for another generation to complete. After all, once the family history has appeared it is likely to arouse some interest on the part of at least one of the younger members of the clan to continue.

If you have maintained an updated mailing list of relatives, much of the initial marketing work for the revision has been accomplished. Yet you must realize that most of the older relatives will not buy the new study, and expertise in selling will have to substitute for the relatively good sale to the family the first time around. This is important to remember, because even if the new edition has undergone relatively few changes, a new bibliography and index will be essential unless the book takes the simple form of a reprint with an appendix of corrections and additions. Some books have been reprinted with marginal notes simply added in black ink to the original camera-ready copy, but customers will appreciate a greater effort.

Experience indicates that the production of the copy for the revised edition should not even begin until all of the first edition has been sold.

It is wise to let people anticipate a little, to let the steam build pressure. All the time *Ancestral Lines Revised* was in preparation, flyers for *Ship Passenger Lists* solicited the names of people who might want a prepublication notice of the new title, and a mailing list of over six hundred names was compiled from these returns. When the book was finally offered at a pre-publication discount of 25%, only one hundred forty orders were received. This was adequate to pay the book manufacturing bill, but did not approach the earlier experience of having about 55% of those requesting their names be put on the pre-publication list actually send their checks in time to receive the discount.

The mailing of new questionnaires to relatives can wait until relatively late in the stage of production of a revised edition. This is not to suggest there will be no delayed returns, but sending a photocopy of the entry in the original edition with a request for new data will result in an improved response. A check of those not responding will show that many failed to simply because they felt their circumstances had not changed enough to warrant it.

If the revised edition is to be left to another member of the family to complete, it would probably be wise to keep the working copy of the book, and the appropriate files and mailing lists, and the original camera-ready copy, with instructions for their use, in a box or cabinet which has been labeled clearly as to its disposition once you are no longer able to supervise the work.

While you will never make a living writing family history the results of having done the work can be most fascinating. The compilation of a book promotes growth in one's stature in the eyes of others. Party conversation seems to develop more easily. Family ties grow. You may inherit immensely interesting collections of family papers from distant relatives. You may be asked if you would like to be listed in a *Who's Who*.

If you have done the family history properly, you have become only a small part of the total work, no more important than any other entry even if your own has been perhaps more complete than most of the others. Yet you will have attained a small measure of immortality as the descendants will always think of you as the member of the family who preserved their heritage.

THOUGHTS ABOUT COMPUTER USE

The first edition of this work was finished entirely on an IBM Selectric which was retired in 1985 when it was sixteen years old. As mentioned earlier, this publisher now uses a Gold Star 286, WordPerfect 5.0 software, and a Hewlett Packard LaserJet IIP, as well as his old Eagle PC with bundled software and a dot matrix printer used to produce drafts and some labels.

Having used a computer, it would be extremely difficult to fail to recommend it highly. The need to key in data will be cut by hundreds of hours, errors in typing repeated drafts will be cut to the bone, and preparation of a revised edition is made simple. Some of the newest printers on the market allow tremendous flexibility in type styles.

A decent computer cost about $5,000 in 1982, while a similar or better one can be purchased, in 1991, for about $650. Thus it is becoming quite practical for anyone doing a major family history or genealogy to consider the purchase of a computer and a laser printer, which can be bought for less than $1,000. These lines are intended to cover some of the basics of computer use. Any detailed consideration of specifics should be left to experts, and if included here would be out-of-date before this book was published.

The computer and printer must be purchased with the book in mind, with the type style a major consideration. A good genealogical type element should include a suitable book face, italics, supernumerals, foreign accent marks, the British pound sign, and the Greek alphabet in both capital and lower case, but no such element exists. It took four IBM elements to find these features for use with a Selectric typewriter, and a compromise may be necessary. However, the reader should consider the question of type first. A computer with sufficient capacity in hard drive can handle soft fonts which will provide great flexibility.

Only one type element was used in the production of earlier editions of this book, an NEC "Super Courier" thimble, which contained more letters, numbers and symbols than can normally be found on a keyboard. Sacrificed were italics (for which bold face or underlining was substituted) and the Greek alphabet, as well as foreign accent marks, although the same type style is available in a variety of languages, including French, German, Spanish, and Swedish. Also sacrificed was the visual ease of typing, as the text had to include a number of computer instructions as well as the basic copy.

As this user became more aware of the versatility of his NEC printer it was easier to change thimbles and accommodate a style similar to that which he enjoyed from a Selectric, with the added bonus of right hand justification, which can be done automatically by the NEC printer, once it has been given the proper instructions (gradually learned by many rereadings of both the computer and printer instruction manuals). The LaserJet proved much simpler to operate, however.

Once the type has been picked you will have picked the printer. Do not do so without seeing examples of type faces. If one store does not have them, go to another.

Once the printer has been selected it is time to consider the software, which should allow you to do whatever you want. If you choose a computer which includes software in a package, it may be much cheaper, but be less efficient. However, many come bundled with excellent software. Friends more familiar with computers may be able to give excellent advice, and help you over the rough parts of learning how to use them.

Thus before you buy, you must know what you wish to do. Do you want to set camera-ready copy and generate mailing labels and invoices? Or do you want to do more? Insist, too, if you are relying on the advice of a salesman, that he demonstrate the ability of the product to do what he says it will do. If the salesman cannot do so, perhaps the manager can.

Do you want a computer to use only at home, or one you can carry around? This researcher is content to do without a portable, and spends his library time making photocopies for use at home rather than pounding away on a keyboard. On the other hand, whichever you want, do make sure it comes with a large memory (several megabytes would be very nice), and two disk drives, or even a hard disk. It is amazing how useful a large memory and plenty of storage can be, particularly when a genealogy can easily contain more than two million characters.

Genealogy House of 3148 Kentucky Avenue South, St. Louis Park, MN 55426-3471, can offer recommendations concerning inexpensive word processing equipment which prints properly the letters of many languages.

A final word. If you have never used a computer before you should still be able to do some word processing within an hour of beginning to read the manual, but eighteen months later you will still be learning how to do more tricks. Yes, there is some pain, and some time wasted, but the one regret is that this publisher did not have a computer long before 1983. Why? It is so much easier to put out a second or third edition of a work when you do not have to retype it from scratch. Even the first edition followed all too many typed drafts. With a computer you simply call your material to the screen from the disk and start making changes. A whole chapter can be altered in minutes rather than days.

APPENDIX

This appendix has grown out of a need which became apparent during the course of the writing of this book. It may interest the reader to know that the first chapter took weeks, and many drafts, while the second chapter took somewhat less effort and the final five, of the first edition, were completed, in rough state, in a glorious five day burst of productivity. As the work took shape from the outline it became clear that there were so many references to the compiler's own work that the public might be saved the considerable expense of buying some of these books if this appendix were to contain sample pages.

It is hoped that any questions of the reader left unanswered by the text can be resolved by inspecting samples which demonstrate how a work should take shape. The makeup of the title page, the copyright page, the preface, the headbands, and the contrast between the color of the cloth and the stamping, as well as every other aspect of this volume, were intended as examples. Careful consideration of each minute part of the work must be given with thought to the effect on sales, the value of the book to the customer, and the preservation of your own reputation as a person marketing something of value.

The "systems schedule" presented in chart form on pages 102 and 103 is intended to summarize visually the contents of the text, and to provide a guide to the use of the index so that you might refer to the text as a reference manual after you have read the entire book.

It is important that each family historian planning to publish develop a schedule for handling the unique problems of that particular project. Thus the material here should be used only as a guide.

Hopefully the remainder of this appendix will be clearly useful, with the reader able to refer to sections of it easily through reference to the table of contents and the index.

SYSTEMS SCHEDULE

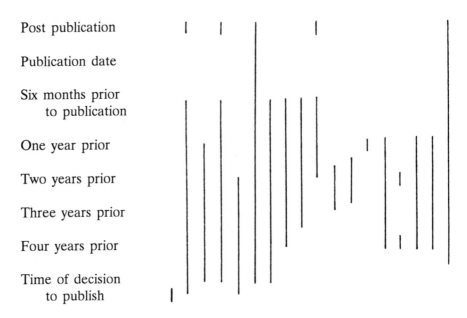

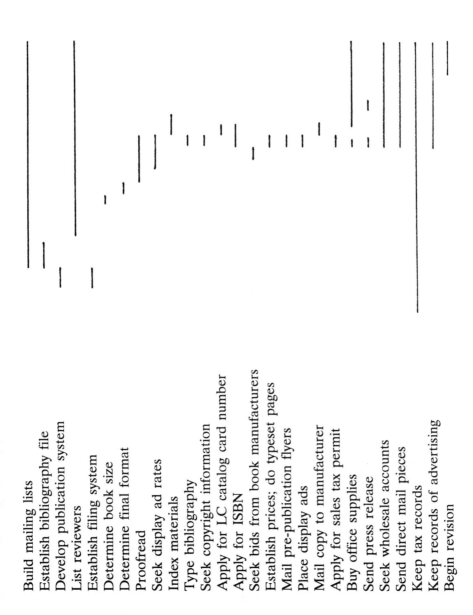

Build mailing lists
Establish bibliography file
Develop publication system
List reviewers
Establish filing system
Determine book size
Determine final format
Proofread
Seek display ad rates
Index materials
Type bibliography
Seek copyright information
Apply for LC catalog card number
Apply for ISBN
Seek bids from book manufacturers
Establish prices; do typeset pages
Mail pre-publication flyers
Place display ads
Mail copy to manufacturer
Apply for sales tax permit
Buy office supplies
Send press release
Seek wholesale accounts
Send direct mail pieces
Keep tax records
Keep records of advertising
Begin revision

The following example of a preface has been modified from the original appearing in *Ancestral Lines Revised*, in that it omits two pages of material anticipating questions concerning the nature of publishing.

PREFACE

No work is perfect, particularly in the field of genealogy, and on the assumption that few will read this preface through the first time they open this book, let it be stated from the beginning that a family history of this size must be used with caution.

Few genealogists have been trained in methods of research. Some cannot write clearly. Thus much which appears in print contains errors of fact, conclusions not warranted by the evidence, or statements easily misunderstood. While my own training in historical research has proven invaluable, and extensive reading of the works of Donald Lines Jacobus and others of nearly equal scholarship has been most instructive, the need to do much research in printed sources requires the admission that some errors must be present. Indeed, this volume contains corrections of some errors which appeared in the first edition of *Ancestral Lines*.

Throughout the text one will note an attempt to analyze critically the sources used. Hopefully the reader will then understand some of the problems faced in the course of compiling this study. Some of the names of the compilers of secondary sources have been indexed, in addition to those of genealogical interest, so that the reader may evaluate for himself the treatment of certain dubious sources listed in the bibliography.

This revision incorporates studies previously presented in *Slade-Babcock Genealogy* and *Ancestral Lines*, with major modifications in format designed to bring together these works into one alphabetical volume complete with corrections and some additions. As both of these volumes have been out of print for more than a year, and, perhaps due to the kindness of reviewers, the demand for them has not abated, it seemed worth|while to do a complete revision.

I cannot honestly say why I have been writing the family history. Farmers intrigue me far more than legislators and *Mayflower* immigrants. Reading detective stories is great fun for some, and genealogy does involve a lot of detective work. It has been fun finding out "who dunnit." The cast of characters is fascinating, including witches, renegades, a notorious triangle, and some known ancestors who lived in caves! Included are Ruth Cook, who married Preserved Fish, and my favorite name now, perhaps, in the personage of Gwynnawg Farfsych.

When I was about twelve my father showed me his copy of the first edition of *American Boyers* along with a letter written by his greatgrandfather from the front lines in Virginia during the Civil War. Thus I became somewhat familiar with my own origins, and continued developing an interest in history which resulted in my entering that profession. In August 1955, at the age of seventeen, I met Townsend Harding Boyer, who introduced me to my Dodge ancestry. Fortunately I took notes and purchased a copy of the *Dodge Genealogy*, for Townsend passed away before I developed a serious interest in family history, and all his materials were lost. Conversations with my mother-in-law led me to do my first real effort in publishing, the Slade-Babcock studies, which became a book only because of the great interest shown by her relatives in sharing and acquiring information on the family tree. In short, I published because I could not make photocopies fast enough.

I was not prepared for the reviews which followed. They, in turn, were responsible for my continuing to publish. One thing led to another. Unfortunately, self-publishing has proven to be a good business, for the attending to all the details has really detracted from genealogical research.

Yet none of this would have been possible without the kind assistance of a great many people, too numerous now to mention in these pages. With the exception of Gwen Boyer Bjorkman of Bellevue, Washington, who was of great help through her correspondence about John Philip[1] Beyer, I believe all have been acknowledged either in previous editions of within the pages of this text.

I would like to answer two questions in the space remaining. The first concerns how to read this book, from the point of view of one not a genealogist. The second deals with how one does publish a book such as this.

This book can be easy to read, and interesting, perhaps, as well, if one remembers that it was not really meant to be read from the beginning to the end. The first step one should take is to find oneself or an ancestor in the index. There may be two or three different pages upon which a typical person may be found. One will be a listing as a child of some couple. A second may be a primary listing with his or her own children. A third may well be an additional mention in connection with other people.

Many will want to read about themselves or their most immediate ancestors first, following with the details of the descendants. Then it is best to follow family lines backwards, one at a time. Each time a male ancestor's wife is found with an asterisk following her maiden name that line can also be followed back. Readers may wish to know that "pedigree charts" may be purchased from many sources for convenience in noting one's own lines.

Further, it will often prove wise to doublecheck the index to see if female ancestors without an asterisk following are not otherwise treated. As an effort has been made to list all of the children of each couple, with their vital records and the names of their spouses, the ancestry of literally thousands of people not treated as primary subjects can be traced.

An explanation of the supernumerals might help. Ella Harriet[8] Talbot, as an example, was a member of the eighth generation of the descendants of the particular immigrant ancestor of the Talbot name, Jared[1] Talbot. Upon her marriage she has been listed as Ella Harriet[8] (Talbot) Boyer, wife of Charles Sumner[7] Boyer, a member of the seventh generation of the Boyer line. Her children included Carl[8] Boyer, a member of the eighth generation of the Boyer line. Her brother, Charles Remington[8] Talbot, had a daughter Gladys[9] Talbot, of the ninth generation of the Talbot line. In all cases where the number of generations from the immigrant ancestor was not known the supernumeral was simply omitted. These numerals are not footnote numbers, but generation numbers. The use of Latin letters in lieu of supernumerals is to denote the generations preceding immigrant ancestors.

Sources and other commentary will be found within brackets within the text. Some will find this data most obtrusive, but frankly the sources are so important, and so often overlooked, that I wanted to make them as obtrusive as possible.

Some of the dates may confuse some readers. The fact is that the people of various countries and colonies have used a variety of calendars. The legal year, historical year, and religious year sometimes began on different dates in the same place. In the English colonies, as well as England, the year began on March 25th until the modern calendar was adopted in 1752. However, January 1st was used to begin the year on the Continent, as well as in the Dutch and Spanish colonies. It is important to understand that an event taking place on 25 February 1690 may have followed by many months an event which had taken place on 28 March 1690. However, in many instances double-dating has been used. Thus the date 25 February 1690/1 refers to an event which may have been listed originally as having happened in 1690, but which according to the modern calendar occurred in 1691. Double dates should occur only for events from 1 January through 24 March. In each case, when consulting original records or *verbatim* transcripts it is necessary to check whether the record keeper changed the year on the first of January or the 25th of March. In the English world practices were most inconsistent, particularly in the eighteenth century.

Now let us turn to the question of publishing a book such as this. I deal with this topic in response to many queries from readers [and the need to fill two more pages, since twelve pages had been reserved in advance of the text].... [Here one should note that the preface, as well as the copyright page, should contain the name and address of the author or compiler, for this is a selling tool for those who see the book in libraries and wish to write for purchase information, as well as to contribute new data.]

Carl Boyer, 3rd

P. O. Box 333
Santa Clarita, California 91322

25 August 1981

Note: The reader may wish to note the ingredients of the preface: 1. an allusion to scholarly approach, 2. comments on project origin and philosophy, 3. explanation of format, 4. any acknowledgements, and 5. such other material as may be necessary for whatever reason.

The following several pages contain the sections on the Frye, Fulwater, Gardner, George, Gifford and Griesemer families from *Ancestral Lines Revised*, with the intent of illustrating how the shorter lineages can be handled.

§ § §

FRYE

George Sherwood's *American Colonists in English Records* contains an abstract of a chancery deposition dated 14 Sept. 1652 in which it is stated that Philippa Fry, deceased, held copyhold in the manor of Combe St. Nicholas in Somerset, England, later held by her daughter, Ann Clarke, for the lives of Ann and George Fry. Sherwood noted that *Somerset and Dorset Notes and Queries*, 18:262, mentioned that Philippa Fry was probably the widow of George Fry, Sr., who was taxed in Combe St. Nicholas in 1620 and died before 1629, and that these were probably the parents of the immigrant, George[1] Frye of Weymouth, Massachusetts Bay [146].

1. GEORGE[A] FRY, SR., was born perhaps in Somerset, England, about 1590, and perhaps died in Combe St. Nicholas, Somerset, before 1629.

If the same man mentioned above, he married Philippa and was taxed in Combe St. Nicholas in 1620. If the same he also had a daughter Ann, who married a Clarke.

Children, of record in Massachusetts Bay:

    2.   i.   George[1], prob. b. Somerset c. 1616; m. (2) Mrs. Mary (--) Brandon.

          ii.   Elizabeth, m. Capt. William Torrey.

    2.   GEORGE[1] FRYE, JR., born probably in or near Combe St. Nicholas, Somerset, England, about 1616, died in Weymouth, Massachusetts Bay, in 1676.

The name of his first wife is unknown. He married second, probably in 1648 or 1649, Mrs. Mary (--) Brandon, widow of William[1] Brandon. It may be possible to identify her through her first husband, who came from Aston Clinton, Buckinghamshire, England, and was son of Thomas Brandon of Puttenham, Bucks. By her first husband she had children Thomas, Sarah, Mary (who married in Weymouth, 11 Nov. 1659, James Smith, Sr.), and Hannah.

George Frye, Jr., was a husbandman and weaver in Weymouth, where he had been an early settler [Waterman]. He was freeman 7 May 1651 [see Shurtleff's *Records of Mass. Bay*, 4:1:459], and deposed on 5 March 1673/4 that he was aged 58 or thereabouts and from Combe St. Nicholas, from which he came to Weymouth in 1640 with the Torrey family. The Sampson has been identified as the ship which brought him to America in an Essex court case involving Capt. William Torrey. He is recorded as saying he knew the Torreys in England [Pope's *Mass. Pioneers*, 177; see Suffolk deeds, 8:392]. However, this compiler has not seen complete documentation of the allegation that his sister was the wife of William Torrey.

His will, dated 6 July 1676 and proven 30 Nov. 1676, gave £5 to his "daughter-in-law" (stepdaughter, that is, the daughter of William and Mary Brandon) Mary, wife of James Smith, Sr., and provided for daughter Ruth Torrey and her son James Smith, daughter Naomi Yeales, and daughter Bethiah Read. James Smith, Sr., of Weymouth, and Timothy Yeales, of Boston, were named executors.

Children, by wife unspecified:

          i.   Ruth[2], m. (1) Joshua Smith, m. (2) Jonathan Torrey.

          ii.   Naomi, m. (?Timothy) Yeales.

Child, by second wife [Waterman]:

    *   iii.   Bethiah, m. c. 1673 John[2] Read.

§ § §

FULWATER

It is possible that Fulwater was an assumed name. No effort has been made to establish a definite point of origin in Flanders.

1. HENRY[B] FULWATER, "born in Lukes and Flanders," according to the record of his apprenticeship in 1571, was buried in the parish of St. Anne, Blackfriars, London, England, 21 Sept. 1605.

He married, probably first, about 1571, Margaret, who was buried at St. Anne, Blackfriars, 25 April 1595. He married second, about 1596, Mary, who was living as late s 6 June 1602. He married third, probably in 1603, Anne, a native of Rouen, France. After his death Anne married in the French Church in Threadneedle Street, London, 11 Feb. 1605/6, Robert De La Tour.

He came to England from the Continent in 1566, possibly from Liège (now in Belgium). He was a member of the London Company of Cutlers, and was made denison (a person with some rights of citizenship) of London about 1572 [Colket]. Described as High German in his apprenticeship papers, he was a Huguenot member of the French Church in London.

Children, by first wife, recorded at St. Anne, Blackfriars:

	i.	Jacob[A], presumed one of two children cited in a 1582 return; m. Martha Irande (or Airley?).
*	ii.	Sarah, bapt. 19 March 1573; m. John[A] Jenckes.
	iii.	John, bur. 7 August 1575.
	iv.	child, bur. 14 June 1576.
	v.	Elizabeth, bur. 15 Oct. 1577.
	vi.	son, bur. 20 Feb. 1580.
	vii.	Isaac, bur. 8 March 1582.
	viii.	Ezekiel, bur. 12 May 1591.
	ix.	Joane, bapt. 6 Oct. 1591; bur. 16 July 1593.
	x.	Mary, bur. 18 July 1593.

Children, by second wife, buried at St. Anne, Blackfriars:

xii.	child, stillborn; bur. 11 April 1597.
xiii.	child, bur. 13 Jan. 1598.

§ § §

GARDNER

This line has been identified mistakenly by Austin as descended from George[1] Gardiner of Newport, Rhode Island [Moriarty].

1.   Lt. SAMUEL[1] GARDNER died in Swanzey (now Swansea), Massachusetts, 8 Dec. 1696.

He married about 1683 Mrs. Elizabeth[2] (Carr*) Brown of Newport, R. I., the widow of James[2] Brown and daughter of Robert[1] Carr. She died 8 Dec. 1697 [Carr].

The time of his arrival in Newport is not known. On 1 Oct. 1687 he bought a four hundred acre farm for £250 in silver from George Lawton of Freetown, Mass. In 1688 he was a selectman of Freetown, then in Plymouth Colony, and in this position he served three years. He was town assessor for two years, town clerk for three years, and treasurer for a year. He was a Deputy to the colonial legislatures of Plymouth and Massachusetts for one year, Plymouth having become a part of Massachusetts in 1691.

He sold his Freetown farm on 14 Nov. 1693 and on 30 Dec. 1693 he bought into what was long known as Gardner's Neck, in Swansea, Mass. He was a selectman of Swansea in 1695 and 1696.

He made a will naming a brother, Robert, and Robert[2] Carr as executors, but the will was not proven legally.

Children of James[2] and Elizabeth[2] (Carr) Brown, surnamed Brown:
     i.   John[3], b. Newport 1671; d. 26 Oct. 1731; m. Elizabeth Cranston.
    ii.   James.
   iii.   Esek.

Children of Samuel[1] and Elizabeth[2] (Carr) (Brown) Gardner:
   iv.   Elizabeth[2], b. 1684; m. Edward Thurston.
    v.   Samuel, b. Newport 28 Oct. 1685; d. 16 Nov. 1768; m. Hannah Smith.
*.   vi.   Martha, b. Newport (recorded in Swansea) 16 Nov. 1686; m. Swansea 23 March 1704 Hezekiah[3] Luther.
  vii.   Patience, b. 30 Oct. 1687.
 viii.   Sarah, m. Samuel Lee.

§ § §

GEORGE

As the information contained in Austin's *Genealogical Dictionary of Rhode Island* has created some confusion concerning the family of Peter[1] George, the compiler found it necessary to consult photocopies of the original records while correcting the data.

1.   PETER[1] GEORGE, born perhaps about 1610, died in New Shoreham, Block Island, Rhode Island, 19 Jan. 1693/4.

He married in Braintree, Massachusetts Bay Colony, about 1642, Mrs. Mary[1] (Rowning*) Ray, widow of Simon[1] Ray. She died also in 1694.

As an "oatmeal maker" from Braintree, he gave a letter of attorney, dated 19 Sept. 1647, concerning the estates of John Rowning and Simon Ray. He bought land in Braintree on 14 May 1648 in partnership with Henry Peale, and sold land there 5 July 1670 [Judd, 5:35; Richardson, *TAG*, 56:96].

In 1660 Block Island was purchased by fourteen persons for £400. When it was settled in 1661 he was assigned lot 16, and with Simon Ray lots 8 and 9. In 1664 he was made freeman and on 26 Oct. 1670 he and four others were appointed to make a rate for the island. In 1676 he was head warden.

His will, which named his friend Joshua Raymond as his executor, was dated 6 Jan. 1691/2 and proven 24 Feb. 1693/4. He mentioned a Negro, "Lango," who was to be freed after serving his wife [1:297-298]. Her will was dated 5 August 1694 and proven 9 Oct. 1694.

Children, born in Braintree:

*   i.   Susan(na)[2], b. Feb. 1642/3; m. Joseph[1] Kent of Swansea.
        ii.   Mary, b. 7 Sept. 1645; m. Edward[1] Ball.
        iii.   Hannah, b. 7 Sept. 1648; m. (1) Tourmet[1] Rose, m. (2) 11 March 1685 James Danielson.
        iv.   John, b. 24 June 1650; d. 9 April 1653.
        v.   Samuel, b. 12 April 1651; m. 20 Dec. 1678 Sarah Rathbone.
        vi.   John, b. 1653; d. young.
        vii.   Peter, b. 9 Jan. 1654/5; d. young.
*   viii. Sarah, b. 4 May 1658; m. 24 April 1674 William[2] Dodge.

§ § §

GIFFORD

The English ancestry of William Gifford is not proven, and his alleged noble lineage has not been substantiated.

1. WILLIAM[1] GIFFORD, born probably in England about 1626, died in Sandwich, Plymouth Colony, 9 April 1687 (when the colony was temporarily under the jurisdiction of the Dominion of New England).

The names of his first two wives are unknown. He married third on 16 July 1683 Mary[2] Mills, who died intestate 10 Feb. 1734 [Daniels, *NEHGR*, 128:241ff.], daughter of John and Sarah Mills of Blackpoint, Mass. (now Scarborough, Maine). A Guilielm Gifford who married 11 Feb. 1635 Elizabeth Grant at St. Martin-in-the-Fields, London, may have been a different man.

Gifford was listed first on 4 Dec. 1647 as owing the estate of Joseph Holiway (or Holloway [q.v.]) 3s. 4d. [Daniels, 242]. He was a member of the Grand Inquest at Plymouth in 1650, and with Thomas Tupper, Thomas Burges, Senr., and Nathaniel Willis was given the power to call a town meeting in Sandwich in 1651. In 1665 he, George[2] Allen, Peter Gaunt and others were among the first proprietors of the Monmouth Patent in New Jersey [C. C. Gardner, *GMNJ*, 16:8]. He stayed in Sandwich, unless perhaps he left temporarily to escape heavy fines for refusing to take the Oath of Fidelity, the first being £5 on 2 Oct. 1658, due to his Quaker practices. He owned land in Sandwich, Falmouth and Dartmouth, and was styled as a "taylor" in deeds from 1670.

The alleged William Gifford of Stamford, Connecticut, was really a Gilford.

Children, by first wife:

    i.   John[2], d. 1708; m. Elishua Crowell [S. Gifford, *NEHGR*, 125:231].

*   ii.   Patience, d. 1673; m. Sandwich 19 Oct. 1665 Richard[2] Kirby.

    iii.   Hananiah, m. Elizabeth; lived N. J. in 1670.

Children, by second wife:

    iv.   William, d. Falmouth 1739; m. (2) 21 June 1711 Lydia Hatch.

    v.   Christopher, b. July 1658; d. 22 Nov. 1748; m. (1) Meribah, m. (2) 1685 Deborah Perry.

    vi.   Robert, b. 1660; d. 1730; m. (1) Sarah Wing, m. (2) Elizabeth.

    v.   Mary (by wife unknown), mentioned 1687.

Children, by third wife:

viii. Jonathan, b. 14 May 1684; m. Lydia.
ix. James, b. 10 March 1685/6; m. 30 March 1710 Deborah Lewis.

§ § §

GRIESEMER

It has been said that this was a family of Huguenots from Alsace, in France [Montgomery, 1713], but the earliest records known, found in Fritz Braun's *Auswanderer aus der Umgebung von Ludwigshafen a Rh. auf dem Schiff "Thistle of Glasgow" 1730* (Neustadt an der Aisch: Buchdruckerei Ph. C. W. Schmidt, 1959), reprinted in German in this compiler's *Ship Passenger Lists: Pennsylvania and Delaware (1641-1825)*, are silent concerning this allegation, which is, no doubt, family tradition.

1. HANS VELTEN[A] GRIESSHEIMER was in Lampertheim, Palatinate Germany, in 1688, when his son Johann Valentine was born.

His wife, Anna Margaretha, has not been identified except in the record of the son listed by Fritz Braun, below.

In Braun's work the symbols * and + are used very frequently, and have been interpreted to mean "baptized" or "christened" and "buried," rather than "born" and "died." The Lampertheim records should reveal more data. It might also be mentioned that the name Griessheimer suggests the family may have originated in Griessheim.

Child, baptized in Lampertheim:
2. i. Johann Valentin[1], bapt. 4 Jan. 1688; d. Hereford Township, Berks County, Pennsylvania, 1759; m. Lampertheim 17 July 1712 Anna Margaretha Andreass.

2. JOHANN VALENTIN[1] GRIESHEIMER, baptized in Lampertheim, Palatinate Germany, 4 Jan. 1688, died in Hereford Township, now in Berks County, Pennsylvania, in 1759.

He married in Lampertheim, 17 July 1712, Anna Margaretha Andreass.

Lampertheim is a village on the left (west) bank of the Rhine, not far north of the French border, which suffered terribly during the long series of wars between the French and the Germans.

Johann Valentin Griesheimer was given his certificate of manumission, his release from serfdom, together with his wife and four children, Casper, Johann, Anna Margaretha and Jakob, on 28 April 1730 by the

Archbishop of Mainz, Frantz Ludwig. In Rotterdam, Holland, he joined the passengers of the *Thistle* of Glasgow, Capt. Colin Dunlop, Master, which left that port in June 1730, cleared with the English authorities at Dover on June 19th, and after a seventy-two day crossing arrived at Philadelphia, Pa., 29 August 1730.

Children, the first six born in Lampertheim, listed by Braun:

- i.   Johann Wilhelm[2], bapt. 17 Sept. 1713; m. Anna Maria. Children: 1. John[3]. 2. Felix, bapt. July 1749. 3. Anna Maria, bapt. 11 July 1752. 4. Catherina, bapt. 12 April 1754. 5. Gertrude, bapt. 29 April 1757. 6. Abraham, b. 1759.
- 3.   ii.   Casper, bapt. 13 March 1715; d. Oley Township, Pa., 1794; m. Rebecca Eshelmann.
- iii.   Anna Margaretha, bapt. 12 Sept. 1719.
- iv.   Jakob, bapt. 27 Feb. 1724.
- v.   Philipp, bapt. 3 Nov. 1725; bur. Lampertheim 1 Feb. 1726.
- vi.   Anna Maria Gerdraut, bapt. May 1728; m. Jakob Gery.
- vii.   Leonard, b. Pennsylvania 1733; d. 1821; m. Elizabeth Faber.

3.   CASPER[2] GRIESEMER, baptized in Lampertheim, Palatinate Germany, 13 March 1715, died in Oley Township, Berks County, Pennsylvania, in 1794, and was buried on his farm.

He married Rebecca Eshelmann [Boyer's *Ship Passenger Lists: Pennsylvania and Delaware*, 130], who was mentioned in his will, which had been dated 23 June 1791.

According to the records of the New Goshenhoppen Reformed Church, the Griesemer family had arrived in Montgomery County by the end of 1730 [Hinke, 14]. Wilhelm, Valadin and Leonhardt Griesemer were all listed as members of the New Goshenhoppen Church in 1738 by the Reverend George Michael Weiss.

His will was recorded in Berks County [*Will Book A*, 293]. His sons John and Peter were executors. The children listed below, in the order of mention in the will, are given according to the custom of listing sons first and daughters last, rather than in birth order.

Children, listed in will [Montgomery, 1422]:

- i.   John[3], executor of father's will.
- ii.   Peter, bur. Oley Township; m. (1) Esther Hoch, dau. of Daniel Hoch, a Swiss, m. (2) Mary Bertolet, of a family from "Kanton Waadt, Schweiz [Switzer-

land], nach Minfeld/Pfalz eingewandert" and then to America [Boyer, 130].

	iii.	Jacob, captain in the Revolution.
	iv.	Valentine, d. before 1791.
	v.	Abraham, d. before 1791.
	vi.	Elizabeth, m. Guldin.
	vii.	Anna Maria, m. Graeff.
	viii.	Anna Margaret, m. Reiter.
	ix.	Susannah.
*	x.	Mary Eva, m. Daniel^2 Ludwig.

Note: The inclusion of the children of Johann Wilhelm^2 Griesemer above is an example of additional data added with the thought of increasing the value of a work to a wider circle of people interested in a certain line. While genealogical research in German is not particularly difficult, many find the sources hard to locate in area libraries.

§ § §

The following Bowen material may be useful as an example of how a more complex presentation would appear in various kinds of type. It has been rewritten, having appeared in different form in the *Plymouth Colony Genealogical Helper*, issue No. 3, in 1975.

BOWEN

A number of published works present data concerning the ancestry of Richard^1 Bowen, but this compiler has not been able to substantiate (or refute) any of the material with references to primary sources. Alice (Mrs. Harold B.) Hove of 1621 Emerson Terrace, Alameda, CA 94501, has surveyed a great number of Bowen sources, however, and made them available to the compiler (1989).

Three generations of Welsh ancestry are given by MacKenzie [*Colonial Families of U. S.*, 3:360], the first being that of Sir James Bowen, whose wife, Mary Hale, was a daughter of Sir John and Margaret Hale. Mary Hale's maternal grandfather was given as Thomas ap Griffith ap Nicholas. Sir James and Mary (Hale) Bowen allegedly had a son, Mathias Bowen, who married Mary Phillips, daughter of John Phillips of Pictou Castle. Their alleged son, James Bowen, married Eleanor Griffith, daughter of John Griffith, Esq., of Richley, and granddaughter of William Griffith, Penrhyn Knight.

A. L. White's *John Barber White* stated that Obadiah[2] Bowen, below, was born in Swansea, Wales, 1 Sept. 1627. The original manuscript of the records of the first Baptist Church at Ilston, Swansea, Wales, kept by John Myles, the pastor, in the Brown University library (where there is also a photostat copy), might shed some light on this question, but the card in the catalog indicates the records date only from 1 August 1649. The book includes Reverend Myles' records in Swansea, Plymouth Colony, to 1669.

Elisha Chandler Bowen's *Memorial of the Bowen Family*, published in Boston by Rand, Avery, and Company, Franklin Press, in 1884, stated that Richard's father, Sir James Bowen, was living in Pembrokeshire, in Llwyngwair, in 1591. It further outlines pedigrees from the Vaughan, Dalton, Stradling [for which see *TAG*, 32:9-12] and Gamage families, with descent from, among others, John of Gaunt and King Edward III. It is said further than a coat of arms on the tombstone of Richard[1] Bowen is further proof of the connection [Dwinnell, 6th leaf]. It is true that Richard was fairly wealthy.

However, E. C. Bowen's own words make obvious the difficulty of proving that Richard[1] Bowen of Rehoboth was the son of James Bowen of Llwyngwair. "I have seen a record somewhere, and noted it, that Richard Bowen of Kittle Hill (who emigrated in 1640) had a son George, his eldest son and heir, whom he left in Wales (and this party was probably the sheriff [of Pembrokeshire] in 1650), and that Hugh and the second George were his descendants.

"It will be borne in mind that Richard Bowen, son of James Bowen of Llwyngwair (living 1591), was among the seventeen children (eighth son), and, when he emigrated (1640), was doubtless over fifty years old, and his eldest son, George, in 1650, was probably thirty years old or more, and, when last sheriff (1679), over sixty. These dates all favor the supposition that George Bowen of Kittle Hill (1650) was the eldest son of Richard Bowen the emigrant.

"While there are discrepancies in the various authorities, I have always taken the most reasonable view..." [E. C. Bowen, 99]. E. C. Bowen stated that "Griffith and George Bowen, immigrants to Boston in 1638, were sons of Owen ap James Bowen of Llwyngwair" [100].

Henry L. P. Beckwith, Jr., Secretary of the Committee on Heraldry of the New England Historic Genealogical Society, has kindly furnished a copy of an application by Richard LeBaron Bowen, an eminent genealogist, dated 21 Feb. 1933, for registration by the committee of the coat of arms that belonged to Richard[1] Bowen, as set forth by Richard LeBaron Bowen. The application was not accepted.

Mr. Beckwith wrote, "It would seem that there is no proof that [Richard[1] Bowen's] gravestone was...cut [with arms claimed by the descendants of Richard Bowen of Rehoboth], but rather that the first proven usage of the arms was on the stone of his great grandson, Dr. Jabez Bowen. I would further note that to the best of my knowledge the ancestry of Richard Bowen is unknown....

"The arms of Griffith Bowen, of Boston, were registered by this Committee. The evidence put forward was a photostat copy of a pedigree drawn up and certified by A. T. Butler, Windsor Herald, back in the twenties." Griffith Bowen's royal ancestry was later documented by Herman Nickerson, Jr. in "Griffith and Margaret (Fleming) Bowen of Wales and Massachusetts" in the *National Genealogical Society Quarterly*, vol. 67 (1979), pp. 163-166, and in "Griffith Bowen of Wales and Massachusetts," *The Connecticut Nutmegger*, 19 (1987), 588-596. As a result Griffith Bowen's line is presented as No. 179 in the sixth edition of Weis' *Ancestral Roots of Sixty American Colonists* (1988). E. C. Bowen said that Griffith Bowen of Boston was said to be from Llangenydd, Wales, because he attended school there [100].

Richard LeBaron Bowen referred to Richard[1] Bowen as "of Glamorganshire, South Wales," with arms, "a stag trippant pierced in the back by an arrow, with crest a stag's head erased." As Mr. Bowen put it, "It is a family tradition that this Coat-of-Arms was cut on the tombstone of the immigrant Richard of Rehoboth, buried in the old Newman Cemetery in February 1674-5. There are in this Cemetery two very old horizontal flat stones supported by foundations, but the action of the elements has obliterated [sic] all cuttings from the tops so that it is impossible to read anything." E. C. Bowen [101] quoted Dwn as saying that Richard, son of James, "chose the hunter's armor, and left the country with it."

The location of other stones which can be identified strongly suggest that these are the ones belonging to Richard Bowen and a wife. The Newman Cemetery, at the southwest corner of the intersection of Newman and Pawtucket Avenues, now in East Providence, R. I., was originally developed in 1668, enlarged in 1680, added to considerably in 1737, and filled out in 1790. It is south, across Newman Avenue, of the Newman Congregational Church.

Mr. Bowen went on to explain that in 1754 Dr. Jabez[4] Bowen buried his wife Huldah in the old Newman Cemetery and had the Bowen arms cut on the stone. At the time Dr. Jabez was sixty years old. "The knowledge of these Arms must have come from his father, Dr. Richard[3], who died when Jabez was 41 years of age. Dr. Richard[3] was about five years old when his father Thomas2 died, and 26 years old when his grandfather the immigrant Richard died.

"In 1790, Mary Bowen, daughter of Jabez[6] wove an elaborate Bowen Coat-of-Arms out of various colored silks and this is still in possession of the family.

"The next appearance of the Bowen Coat-of-Arms is on the tombstone of Deputy Governor Jabez[6] Bowen, buried in Swan Point Cemetery in Providence, R. I. He was 41 years of age when his greatuncle Jabez[4] died, and 73 years of age at the death of his father Ephraim[5], who was brought up from the age of nine by his uncle Jabez[4].

"On this tombstone it is especially set forth that Jabez[6] is *the fifth in descent...from Richard Bowen who emigrated from Glamorganshire in South Wales, A. D. 1640....* This is especially significant in view of the fact that we now know there are several different Bowen Coat-of-Arms. This must have been known to him and have been the reason for the special reference to the ancestor."

Mr. Bowen then quotes from page three of Edwin A. Bowen's *The Bowens of Woodstock*, "There was an ancient family of Bowens of Court House, in the parish of Ilston, but I have not been able to connect it with that of the Bowens of Slade; this is a rather singular thing; the peninsula of Gower is a comparatively small locality, and it would be very strange if the two families should be distinct.... The Arms of those of Bowen of Slade are those of Griffith Gwyr, namely, a stag lodged, holding an oak branch in his mouth; while those of Bowen of Court House are a stag, trippant with an arrow stuck in his back..." [illustrated in *Matthew's American Armory and Blue Book* (London, 1908), 11].

Richard LeBaron Bowen then concluded that Jabez[4] Bowen was "in an exceptional position" to know of Bowen arms, and that with the exception of Thomas[2] Bowen, about whom little is known, all the Bowens mentioned were well educated, four being doctors and one a deputy governor.

A number of colonial arms were discussed in *Rhode Island Historical Collections*, where it was noted that "Burke gives 'Azure a stag argent with an arrow stuck in the back and attired or' for the Bowens of Kittle Hill and Swansea, co. Glamorgan, but with a different crest. Burke also gives a variant coat 'Gules a stag trippant argent pierced in the back with an arrow and attired or' as granted in 1812 to the Bowens of Milford, co. Mayo. The crest is different, and the change of the field from azure to gules was evidently 'for difference.'" These arms are illustrated in the reprint collection, *Genealogies of Rhode Island Families from Rhode Island Periodicals* (Baltimore, 1983), volume 2, pages 697-698.

It is rather curious then that Richard LeBaron Bowen's exceptional history of Rehoboth in four volumes did not make mention of this theory, unless he had rejected it by 1940. Such may well be the case.

The most fanciful tale of the Bowen ancestry appears in Lester C. Gustin's *The Ancestry of Herbert E. Gustin and his wife Julia L. Carlisle and Their Descendants* (2 volumes, 1954). In short, Richard[1] Bowen is listed in descent in the fortieth generation from Beli Mawr, who was given as King of Britain in 55 B. C. Gustin stated that Richard's father was Thomas Bowen of Court House, who died in 1587, son of Harry Thomas Bowen of Court House, who also died in 1587, son of Theodore Bowen, who was in turn son of Harry Bowen of Court House, whose will was dated 4 July 1467, one hundred and twenty years before! The dates alone are enough to cause one to be suspicious. John S. Wurts in *Magna Charta*, part VIII (1959), published this line without the offending dates, allowing eighteen generations of descent from Teudor Mawr, who was killed in battle in 993, to Richard[1] Bowen, who died in 1674/5 [pp. 2630-31, 2926]. Charles H. Browning's *Americans of Royal Descent*, 6th ed. (Philadelphia, 1905) presents the line with more questionable dates [pp. 462-63].

1. RICHARD[1] BOWEN, born, according to tradition, in Glamorganshire, South Wales, died in Rehoboth, Plymouth Colony, and was buried there 4 Feb. 1674/5 [1:52].

It is said his first wife was named Ann. He married second, in Hingham, Plymouth Colony, or Weymouth [C. Fuller], Nov. 1648, Mrs. Elizabeth (Rey) Marsh, who was buried in Rehoboth in 1675. She was the widow of George Marsh, who died in Hingham 2 July 1647 [Bowen, 2:13]; she had been born in Hempstead, England, married in 1623, and came to America on the *Blessing* in 1635 [see *Desc. of John Page*, 106-107].

Clarence C. Fuller's excellent *Record of Robert Fuller* (1969) quotes the *History of Weymouth* in describing the "earliest land record of Richard[1] Bowen," dated 1642: "Tenn acres Eyght of them upland two of swampe lying in the plaine first given to Thomas White bounded on the East with the land of Martin Phillipes, of Ralph (Allin) on the west, of his owne on the south, a highway on the north.

"Two acres of upland and salt marsh first given to Tho White bounded on the East with the comon, on the west with the land of Ralph Allin, on the north with his owne land, on the south with John Uphams marsh.

"Two acres first giuen to John King bounded on the East west & north with his owne land and of Mr. Newman on the south."

Mr. Fuller believed this meant that Richard Bowen was a permanent settler of Weymouth, so far as his intentions in 1642 were concerned, but he was soon one of the first settlers at Seekonk, later Rehoboth, with his estate valued at an above average £270.

Earlier, A. L. White had suggested that Richard Bowen was in Boston and Salem (while not mentioning Weymouth) before going to Rehoboth, where he was listed as a proprietor in 1643 and as freeman 4 June 1645. Rehoboth's first Board of Selectmen chosen 9 Dec. 1644 included Alexander Winchester, Richard Wright, Henry Smith, Edward Smith, Walter Palmer, William Smith, Stephen Paine, Richard Bowen and Robert Martin.

He was of record 20 or 29 Dec. 1645 with Robert Martin and Stephen Paine as the three "layed out yt necke of land called knowne by the name of Wanomoycet," and on 16 March 1645/6 he was appointed with Robert Titus, William Smith, Capt. Richard Wright, Alexander Winchester, Thomas Bliss, Stephen Paine and Thomas Cooper to get the fences in Rehoboth in order by the 23rd of the month. He was elected townsman (selectman) again on 26 May 1647 with Mr. Browne, Mr. Peck, Stephen Paine, Mr. Winchester, William Carpenter and Edward Smith [Bowen, 1:28, 3:121 and 142].

On 13 May 1653 "Richard Bowen & James Ridwaye" were chosen "for overseers of the wayes," and a list of "the Subscriptions of the Inhabitants" of Rehoboth empowering Richard Bowen, Stephen Paine, Thomas Cooper and William Sabin to represent them in settling the status of Rehoboth lands lying within the bounds of the new Sowams purchase was drawn up on June 1653 [Bowen, 1:18 and 126].

In the spring of 1654 it was found necessary to appoint William Carpenter, Richard Bowen and John Allen as arbitrators in a dispute between Richard Titus and Nicholas Ide over a parcel of salt meadow [Bowen, 2:138]. In 1671 Richard Bowen was recorded as having been assessed 3/7 in taxes, a figure somewhat below the median, and by 28 May 1672 he was recorded as having sold his one-half share in the 1666 North Purchase distribution to Thomas Ormsbee [Bowen, 1:39 and 41].

His signature on his will was a mark, even though he was literate, probably because he was too sick to write his name [Bowen, 1:111]. The will was proven 4 June 1675. The inventory totaled £175.15s.8d. His daughter Ruth "Kenericke" inherited one mare, one colt and a pewter platter.

Children, by first wife:

    i.   Sarah[2], killed by Indians, bur. Rehoboth 14 Oct. 1676; m. 23 April 1647 Robert[1] Fuller.

    ii.   Alice, m. Salem, Mass., 1636, Robert[1] Wheaton.

    iii.   Ruth, bur. Rehoboth 31 Oct. 1688 [1:89]; m. there 23 April 1647 George[1] Kendrick.

2.	iv.	Obadiah, d. c. 1710; m. Mary.
3.	v.	Thomas, d. c. 1663; m. Elizabeth.
	vi.	William, bur. Rehoboth 10 March 1686/7 [1:57].
4.	vii.	Richard, m. Rehoboth 4 March 1646 Esther Sutton, m. possibly (2) Rehoboth 20 Jan. 1689/90 Martha Saben.

2. OBADIAH[2] BOWEN made a will dated 11 Dec. 1708, which was probated 14 Oct. 1710 [*MD*, 18:204-209].

His wife Mary has been identified variously as a Clifton, Chilton or Titus.

It is interesting to note that an Obadiah Bowen (another person) was licensed to sell wines and strong waters at Gloucester, Mass., in 1638 [see *Essex Antiquarian*, 2:35].

Obadiah's will mentioned four granddaughters in addition to others, the granddaughters being Katherine, Sarah, Alice and Elizabeth or Mary, alias Bush.

Children, the first ten recorded in Rehoboth [1:27]:

5.	i.	Obadiah[3], b. 18 Sept. 1651; d. 11 July 1699 [1:93]; m. Abigail.
	ii.	Mary, b. 18 Jan. 1652/3; m. Rehoboth [1:43] 30 May 1673 Isaac Allen, perhaps m. (2) Ephraim Smith.
	iii.	Sara, b. 6 Nov. 1654; m. Rehoboth [1:45] John Savage.
6.	iv.	Samuel, b. 16 Nov. 1659; d. Salem Co., N. J., 21 Jan. 1728/9; m. Swansea 26 May 1684 Elizabeth (Wood) Wheaton.
7.	v.	Joseph, b. 26 June 1662; m. Elizabeth[2] Round.
8.	vi.	Thomas, b. 3 August 1664; m. 17 June 1689 Thankful Mason.
	vii.	Hannah, b. 3 May 1665; m. Timothy Brooks; lived Cohanze (Cohansey), Salem Co., N. J.
	viii.	Lydia, b. 23 April 1666; m. Joseph Mason.
	ix.	Marcy, b. 18 March 1672.
	x.	Isaac, b. 30 Sept. 1674.
	xi.	Hezekiah (mentioned in father's will), m. (int. Rehoboth 15 June) 1706 Elizabeth London of Swansea, Mass.
	xii.	James (mentioned in father's will), perhaps the James Bowen who m. Rehoboth [1:169] 6 May 1703 Elizabeth Garnzey.

3. THOMAS[2] BOWEN, perhaps born in Wales, probably died in Rehoboth, Plymouth Colony, in 1663, after he made his will there on 11 April of that year.

His wife Elizabeth, who he may have married in Essex County, Mass., was mentioned in his will and married second the Reverend Samuel[2] Fuller of Middleborough. She died in Plympton, Mass., 11 Nov. 1713. Research into the Prentices of New London, Connecticut, might provide her identity, for in 1667 she gave a power of attorney, as the sometime wife of Thomas Bowen, late of Rehoboth, and Samuel Fuller of Plymouth, to their brother-in-law John Prentice of New London, blacksmith, to sell Thomas Bowen's land in New London [Charles Shepard, "Bowen Family Notes," 141]. She has also been identified as a Nichols, daughter of Francis[3], John[2].

The Thomas Bowen who appeared as a witness 27 Oct. 1642 in Essex County, Massachusetts Bay [see *Records and Files of the Quarterly Court of Essex County*, 1:47], was fined in Salem in 1647, and was apparently a planter and fisherman in Marblehead, Mass., from 1642 to 1681 or later [Perley's *Hist. Salem*; Shepard, 140], was a different man. Administration on his estate was granted in 1705, according to Pope's *Pioneers*. This Thomas also was married to an Elizabeth.

Thomas[2] Bowen moved to Rehoboth in his later years, after having lived in New London, Conn., from about 1657 to 1662. His will mentioned wife Elizabeth and his son Richard, and named his brother-in-law Robert[1] Fuller and his brother Obadiah[2] Bowen as executors [*MD*, 16:128].

The Rehoboth records [1:2] contain entries recording the births of two Bowen children, Richard born August 16--, and Abigail born Dec. 16--, not otherwise identified.

Child, mentioned in his will:

9.	i.	Richard[3], m. Rehoboth 9 Jan. 1683 Mercy[3] Titus.
	ii.	Abijah, m. Middleborough, Mass., 1683, Abigail Wood.

4. RICHARD[2] BOWEN lived in Rehoboth, Plymouth Colony.

He married in Rehoboth, 4 March 1646 [1:44], Esther Sutton. Possibly he married second, in Rehoboth, 20 Jan. 1689/90 [1:49] Martha Saben, who was perhaps the same as "Martha Bowen" recorded at Rehoboth [2:242] as born 10 Jan. 1644/5 and died 11 Jan. 1734/5.

Children, of Richard and Esther, born in Rehoboth [3R; 1:2]:

	i.	Sarah[3], b. 7 Feb. [A. L. White, 248] 1656; d. Rehoboth 14 May 1704 [GS, cited in Abell, 47]; m. Reserved[2] Abell.

	ii.	Hester, b. 20 April 1660; d. Rehoboth 26 Feb. 1701 [1:179]; an Esther Bowen m. there [1:47] 20 July 1682 Samuel Miller.
10.	iii.	Richard, b. 17 Jan. 1662; m. there [1:94] 28 Feb. 1690/1 Patience Peck.
	iv.	Mary, b. 5 Oct. 1666; perhaps m. there [1:48] 31 Dec. 1687 Philip Walker.
11.	v.	John, b. 15 March 167- [1:2]; m. there [1:168] 12 Sept. 1700 Elizabeth Beckett.

5. OBADIAH³ BOWEN, born in Rehoboth, Plymouth Colony, 18 Sept. 1651, died there, when in Massachusetts, 11 July 1699 [1:93].

His wife's name was Abigail. Obadiah² Bowen, her father-in-law, mentioned Abigail's daughter Sarah in his will, dated in 1708. Did Abigail marry second, in Rehoboth [1:168], 1 July 1701, Benjamin Fiske, or was she the Abigail Bowen who married John² Round of Swansea?

Children, born in Rehoboth [1:83]:

    i.   Aron⁴, b. 6 Nov. 169- (Aaron).
    ii. Sarah, b. 5 Nov. 169- (also "Daniel").
    iii. Nathan, b. 4 April 1698.

6. SAMUEL³ BOWEN, born in Rehoboth, Plymouth Colony, died in Salem County, New Jersey, 21 Jan. 1728/9.

He married in Swansea, Plymouth Colony, 26 May 1684, Elizabeth (Wood) Wheaton [letter from Fern B. Christensen of 1017 Oma Street, Natchitoches, LA 71457, dated 31 August 1983].

Children, recorded in Rehoboth [1:65]:

    i.   Samuel⁴, b. 1 Jan. 1687/8.
    ii. Dan, b. 1 August 1690.
    iii. Elijah, b. 4 August 1695.
    iv. Joanna, b. 1 Dec. 1696.

7. JOSEPH³ BOWEN was born in Rehoboth, Plymouth Colony, 26 June 1662.

His wife was Elizabeth² Round [Bristol Co., Mass., Probate, 3:299].

The compiler has been told [source not given] that a receipt signed by one Jacob Chase reads, "January ye 6: 1711 this is to signify that Allice the Daughter of Joseph Bowen the wife of Jacob Chase hath Recd a pewter plattr which was given to her by her Honored Grandfather in his last will." The probate records of the estate of Obadiah² Bowen name Alice as a granddaughter, but no "Alice" was found among the children listed in the Rehoboth records of births.

Children, born in Rehoboth [1:49]:

i.   John⁴, b. 26 Sept. 1689.
ii.   Ruth, b. 15 Oct. 1691.
iii.   Elisha, b. 6 July 1693.
iv.   Obadiah, b. 7 July 1695.
v.   Naoma, b. 9 Sept. 1697; d. Rehoboth 13 July 1699 [1:181].
vi.   Joseph, b. 9 Nov. 1699.
vii.   Jabish, b. 23 Nov. 1701.
viii.   Elizabeth, b. 6 June 1704.
ix.   Mary, b. 1 July 1706.
x.   Alice, alleged daughter, m. to Jacob Chase by 6 Jan. 1711.

8. THOMAS³ BOWEN, born in Rehoboth, Plymouth Colony, 3 August 1664, left a will dated 25 Dec. 1730 which was probated 21 June 1743.

He married 17 July 1689 Thankful Mason, who was living in 1743, according to the probate records of her husband's estate.

Children, the first four recorded in Rehoboth [1:84], with the rest listed in their father's will and probate records:

i.   Josiah⁴, b. 1 Oct. 1691.
ii.   Mary, b. 30 Nov. 1693; m. Gilbert Seamens.
iii.   Isaac, b. 3 Nov. [Jan.?] 1695/6 [sic].
iv.   Stephen, b. 16 Jan. 1697/8; m. 17 Oct. 1723 Phebe³ Slade.
v.   Hannah, m. Charles Seamens.
vi.   Samuel, m. Sarah Smith.
vii.   Nathaniel.
viii.   Richard, b. 21 Jan. 1704; m. 13 Dec. 1733 Remember⁴ Goodspeed [Austin, 6].
ix.   Marcy, m. Jan. 1716/7 Nathan⁴ Luther [L. L. Luther's *The Luther Family in America* (1976), 102].
x.   John.
xi.   Katherine, m. Curtis.

9. RICHARD³ BOWEN, born about 1650 (the entry in Rehoboth records [1:2] for August 16-- may apply here), lived in Rehoboth, Massachusetts, which town was earlier under the jurisdiction of Plymouth Colony and the Dominion of New England. When and where he and his wife died has not been found, although Dwinnell stated he died in 1736.

He married in Rehoboth, 9 Jan. 1683 [1:48], Mercy³ Titus.

According to various sources he was five or thirteen years old when his father died. He was a medical doctor.

Children, born in Rehoboth [1:57], listed as children "of Richard (of Thomas)":

* i. Elizabeth[4], b. 11 Nov. 1684; m. (1) Rehoboth 10 Dec. 1706 Enoch[4] Hunt, m. (2) there 2 Dec. 1711 James[4] Brown of Swansea.

ii. Abijah, b. 10 April 1687; m. Rehoboth [1:176] 2 June 1708 Potter Hunt.

iii. Thomas, b. 20 August 1689; m. Rehoboth [1:177] 8 August 1720 Sarah[4] Hunt (of Ephraim[3], Peter[2], Enoch[1]).

iv. Damaries, b. 26 April 1692; m. Rehoboth [1:157] 18 June 1713 Stephen[4] Hunt.

v. Jabesh, b. 19 Oct. 1696; m. Rehoboth [2:134] 30 Jan. 1717/8 Huldah Hunt; mentioned in the introduction above as the Dr. Jabez Bowen who claimed the Bowen coat-of-arms.

vi. Ebenezer, b. 23 August 1699; m. Rehoboth [2:138] by Rev. John Greenwood 17 June 1724 to Anne Newman.

vii. Urania, b. 23 Sept. 1707; m. Rehoboth [2:148] by Rev. John Greenwood 4 March 1736/7 to John Bush.

10. RICHARD[3] BOWEN was born in Rehoboth, Plymouth Colony, 17 Jan. 1662, and continued to live there.

He married there [1:94], 28 Feb. 1690/1, Patience Peck.

Children, listed tentatively:

i. Christopher[4], b. 7 April 1691.

ii. Ichabod.

iii. Dan.

iv. Mary.

v. Peter.

vi. Eber.

vii. Richard, b. 19 June 1702; d. young.

viii. Richard, b. 24 March 1703/4; d. Rehoboth 11 July 1706 [1:173].

ix. Zerviah, b. 16 Nov. 1706.

x. Uriall, b. 9 July 1709.

xi. David, b. 1 August 1714.

11. JOHN[3] BOWEN, born in Rehoboth, Plymouth Colony, 15 March 167- [1:2], may have lived in a part of town set off to another town.
He married in Rehoboth, 12 Sept. 1700 [1:168], Elizabeth Beckett.
Children, born in Rehoboth:

i.	Peter[4], b. 22 July 1701; d. 9 July 1748 [A. L. White, 249]; m. 23 March 1727 Susannah Kent.
ii.	Elizabeth, b. 17 July 1702; m. 14 Sept. 1726 Caleb Lamb of Barrington, Mass. (later in R. I.).
iii.	Sarah, b. 27 Sept. 1704; m. 9 May 1728 William Whipple of Attleboro, Mass.
iv.	Esther, b. 9 Dec. 1706.
v.	John, b. 19 Dec. 1709; m. (1) 5 Feb. 1736 Mary Reed [A. L. White, 249], m. (2) 17 August 1749 Hannah Peck, m. (3) 3 May 1759 Mary Ormsbee.

§ § §

BIBLIOGRAPHY

The following printed works were consulted by the compiler during the course of the research on this line. This list is not exhaustive; it merely indicates what research need not be covered again by those doing more intensive study.

Abell, Horace A., and Lewis P. Abell. *The Abell Family in America; Robert Abell of Rehoboth, Mass., His English Ancestry and His Descendants.* Rutland, Vermont: The Tuttle Publishing Company, Inc., 1940.

Austin, John Osborne. *American Authors' Ancestry.* Providence, 1915.

Bowen, Edward Augustus. "Griffith Bowen of Boston," *New England Historical and Genealogical Register,* 47 (1893), 453-459.

Bowen, E[lisha] C[handler]. *Memorial of the Bowen Family.* 1884.

Bowen, Richard LeBaron. *Early Rehoboth: Documented Historical Studies of Families and Events in This Plymouth Colony Township,* 4 vols. Rehoboth, Mass., 1945-1950.

"Bowen Genealogy," *The Essex Antiquarian,* 10 (1906), 57-58 [Nathan[1] Bowen of Marblehead, Mass.].

[Bowman, George Ernest.] "Plymouth Colony Wills and Inventories: Thomas Bowen's Will," *Mayflower Descendant*, 16 (1914), 128.

Bowman, George Ernest. "The Wills of Obadiah and Thomas Bowen," *Mayflower Descendant*, 18 (1916), 204-210.

Fuller, Clarence C. *Records of Robert Fuller of Salem and Rehoboth and Some of His Descendants*. Norwood, Mass., 1969.

Gustin, Lester C. *The Ancestry of Herbert E. Gustin and his wife Julia L. Carlisle and Their Descendants*, 2 vols. 1954.

Nickerson, Herman, Jr. "Griffith and Margaret (Fleming) Bowen of Wales and Massachusetts," *National Genealogical Society Quarterly*, 67 (1979), 163-166.

Nickerson, Herman, Jr. "Griffith Bowen of Wales and Massachusetts," *The Connecticut Nutmegger*, 19 (1987), 588-596.

Perley, Sidney. "Beverages in the Old Days," *The Essex Antiquarian*, 2 (1898), 33-37.

Shepard, Charles. "Bowen Family Notes" in *Genealogies of Rhode Island Families*, 2 vols. Baltimore: Genealogical Publishing Co., Inc., 1983 [pp. 139-141].

Weis, Frederick Lewis. *Ancestral Roots of Sixty Colonists Who Came to New England between 1623 and 1650*, 6th ed. Baltimore: Genealogical Publishing Co., Inc., 1988.

White, A. L. *Ancestors and Descendants of John Barber White*. 1913 [photocopies, citation from Tuttle catalog #376].

§ § §

Once the text has been typed entirely you will have to consider materials which have been contributed too late for inclusion in the text proper. The following example of an Appendix contains excerpts of that from *Ancestral Lines Revised*. The appendix should not be typed until the index draft has been completed for the text. Then additional names in the appendix can be added to the index just prior to the typing of that section.

All of the material above was set in Bitstream Dutch Roman 12 Point type using WordPerfect 5.0 processing and an HP II laser printer. The original camera ready copy was then reduced to 88% of the original size. The following is an example of some of the same material set in Courier 10 Pitch with continuation of right hand justification.

BOWEN

A number of published works present data concerning the ancestry of Richard[1] Bowen, but this compiler has not been able to substantiate (or refute) any of the material with references to primary sources. Alice (Mrs. Harold B.) Hove of 1621 Emerson Terrace, Alameda, CA 94501, has surveyed a great number of Bowen sources, however, and made them available to the compiler (1989).

Three generations of Welsh ancestry are given by MacKenzie [Colonial Families of U. S., 3:360], the first being that of Sir James Bowen, whose wife, Mary Hale, was a daughter of Sir John and Margaret Hale. Mary Hale's maternal grandfather was given as Thomas ap Griffith ap Nicholas. Sir James and Mary (Hale) Bowen allegedly had a son, Mathias Bowen, who married Mary Phillips, daughter of John Phillips of Pictou Castle.   Their alleged son, James Bowen, married Eleanor Griffith, daughter of John Griffith, Esq., of Richley, and granddaughter of William Griffith, Penrhyn Knight.

A. L. White's John Barber White stated that Obadiah[2] Bowen, below, was born in Swansea, Wales, 1 Sept. 1627. The original manuscript of the records of the first Baptist Church at Ilston, Swansea, Wales, kept by John Myles, the pastor, in the Brown University library (where there is also a photostat copy), might shed some light on this question, but the card in the catalog indicates the records date only from 1 August 1649. The book includes Reverend Myles' records in Swansea, Plymouth Colony, to 1669.

Elisha Chandler Bowen's Memorial of the Bowen Family, published in Boston by Rand, Avery, and Company, Franklin Press, in 1884, stated that Richard's father, Sir James Bowen, was living in Pembrokeshire, in Llwyngwair, in 1591. It further outlines pedigrees from the Vaughan, Dalton, Stradling [for which see TAG, 32:9-12] and Gamage families, with descent from, among others, John of Gaunt and King Edward III. It is said further than a coat of arms on the tombstone of Richard[1] Bowen is further proof of the connection

[Now an example of Courier 10 Pitch with a ragged right margin:]

[Dwinnell, 6th leaf]. It is true that Richard was
fairly wealthy.
     However, E. C. Bowen's own words make obvious the
difficulty of proving that Richard[1] Bowen of Rehoboth
was the son of James Bowen of Llwyngwair. "I have
seen a record somewhere, and noted it, that Richard
Bowen of Kittle Hill (who emigrated in 1640) had a
son George, his eldest son and heir, whom he left in
Wales (and this party was probably the sheriff [of
Pembrokeshire] in 1650), and that Hugh and the second
George were his descendants.
     "It will be borne in mind that Richard Bowen, son
of James Bowen of Llwyngwair (living 1591), was among
the seventeen children (eighth son), and, when he
emigrated (1640), was doubtless over fifty years old,
and his eldest son, George, in 1650, was probably
thirty years old or more, and, when last sheriff
(1679), over sixty. These dates all favor the supposition that George Bowen of Kittle Hill (1650) was
the eldest son of Richard Bowen the emigrant.
     "While there are discrepancies in the various
authorities, I have always taken the most reasonable
view..." [E. C. Bowen, 99]. E. C. Bowen stated that
"Griffith and George Bowen, immigrants to Boston in
1638, were sons of Owen ap James Bowen of Llwyngwair"
[100].
     Henry L. P. Beckwith, Jr., Secretary of the Com-
mittee on Heraldry of the New England Historic Genealogical Society, has kindly furnished a copy of an
application by Richard LeBaron Bowen, an eminent
genealogist, dated 21 Feb. 1933, for registration by
the committee of the coat of arms that belonged to
Richard[1] Bowen, as set forth by Richard LeBaron
Bowen. The application was not accepted.
     Mr. Beckwith wrote, "It would seem that there is
no proof that [Richard[1] Bowen's] gravestone was...cut
[with arms claimed by the descendants of Richard
Bowen of Rehoboth], but rather that the first proven
usage of the arms was on the stone of his great
grandson, Dr. Jabez Bowen. I would further note that
to the best of my knowledge the ancestry of Richard
Bowen is unknown....
     "The arms of Griffith Bowen, of Boston, were
registered by this Committee. The evidence put
forward was a photostat copy of a pedigree drawn up
and certified by A. T. Butler, Windsor Herald, back
in the twenties." Griffith Bowen's royal ancestry
was later documented by Herman Nickerson, Jr. in

[Here it should be noted that the type in Dutch Roman 12 Point takes twelve per cent less space, vertically, than the Courier 10 Pitch to present the same amount of narrative material.]

Departing from the Bowen narrative, let us compare how the children of Richard[1] Bowen look in different types, all reduced to 88% of the size prepared on the camera-ready copy.

Dutch Roman 12 Point, justified margins:
Children, by first wife:
        i.   Sarah[2], killed by Indians, bur. Rehoboth 14 Oct. 1676; m. 23 April 1647 Robert[1] Fuller.
        ii.   Alice, m. Salem, Mass., 1636, Robert[1] Wheaton.
        iii. Ruth, bur. Rehoboth 31 Oct. 1688 [1:89]; m. there 23 April 1647 George[1] Kendrick.
2.   iv. Obadiah, d. c. 1710; m. Mary.
3.   v.   Thomas, d. c. 1663; m. Elizabeth.
        vi. William, bur. Rehoboth 10 March 1686/7 [1:57].
4.   vii. Richard, m. Rehoboth 4 March 1646 Esther Sutton, m. possibly (2) Rehoboth 20 Jan. 1689/90 Martha Saben.

Dutch Roman 10 Point, justified margins:
Children, by first wife:
        i.   Sarah[2], killed by Indians, bur. Rehoboth 14 Oct. 1676; m. 23 April 1647 Robert[1] Fuller.
        ii.   Alice, m. Salem, Mass., 1636, Robert[1] Wheaton.
        iii. Ruth, bur. Rehoboth 31 Oct. 1688 [1:89]; m. there 23 April 1647 George[1] Kendrick.
2.   iv. Obadiah, d. c. 1710; m. Mary.
3.   v.   Thomas, d. c. 1663; m. Elizabeth.
        vi. William, bur. Rehoboth 10 March 1686/7 [1:57].
4.   vii. Richard, m. Rehoboth 4 March 1646 Esther Sutton, m. possibly (2) Rehoboth 20 Jan. 1689/90 Martha Saben.

Courier 10 Pitch, justified margins:
Children, by first wife:
        i.   Sarah[2], killed by Indians, bur. Rehoboth 14 Oct. 1676; m. 23 April 1647 Robert[1] Fuller.
        ii.   Alice, m. Salem, Mass., 1636, Robert[1] Wheaton.
        iii. Ruth, bur. Rehoboth 31 Oct. 1688 [1:89]; m. there 23 April 1647 George[1] Kendrick.
2.   iv. Obadiah, d. c. 1710; m. Mary.

3.   v.   Thomas, d. c. 1663; m. Elizabeth.
       vi.   William, bur. Rehoboth 10 March 1686/7
             [1:57].
4.   vii.   Richard, m. Rehoboth 4 March 1646 Esther
             Sutton, m. possibly (2) Rehoboth 20
             Jan. 1689/90 Martha Saben.

Courier 10 Pitch, right ragged margin:
   Children, by first wife:
        i.   Sarah^2, killed by Indians, bur.
             Rehoboth 14 Oct. 1676; m. 23 April
             1647 Robert^1 Fuller.
       ii.   Alice, m. Salem, Mass., 1636, Robert^1
             Wheaton.
      iii.   Ruth, bur. Rehoboth 31 Oct. 1688
             [1:89]; m. there 23 April 1647
             George^1 Kendrick.
2.   iv.   Obadiah, d. c. 1710; m. Mary.
3.   v.   Thomas, d. c. 1663; m. Elizabeth.
       vi.   William, bur. Rehoboth 10 March 1686/7
             [1:57].
4.   vii.   Richard, m. Rehoboth 4 March 1646
             Esther Sutton, m. possibly (2)
             Rehoboth 20 Jan. 1689/90 Martha
             Saben.

Thus on the original camera-ready copy of this book the Dutch Roman 12 Point presentation of the children occupied about 2.3" vertically, the Dutch Roman 10 Point about 1.75", the justified Courier 10 Pitch 2.67", and the Courier 10 Pitch with the ragged right margin 2.84".

Vertical inches are money in that the fewer vertical inches the fewer pages. Saving some pages in a book can bring about a substantial decrease in costs. However, you should never sacrifice readability. The versatility found in using a computer instead of a typewriter, however, should be obvious.

§ § §

Once the text has been typed entirely you will have to consider materials which have been contributed too late for inclusion in the text proper. The following example of an Appendix contains excerpts of that from *Ancestral Lines Revised*. The appendix should not be typed until the index draft has been completed for the text. Then additional names in the appendix can be added to the index just prior to the typing of that section.

APPENDIX

Insofar as was possible, research and correspondence continued throughout the revision of this work, and was incorporated into the text as much as possible, even when extensive retyping was required to accommodate further revisions.   However, some correspondence was delayed due to the need for obtaining new addresses and the forwarding of mail, and the results are given below. In addition, new materials not involving corrections have been included below where convenience dictated. All of the following material has been indexed.

BABCOCK - Darby G. Livingston, C.G.R.S., of Box 487, Bennington, VT 05201, has contributed the following burial records from gravestones in Alburg, Vermont:
Center Cemetery:
Thomas Babcock, 1818 - July 22nd 1864, buried in Andersonville, Ga.,
     his wife Sophronia Darrow, 1819 - Feb. 25th, 1897.
Job Babcock, Sept. 4th 1811 - May 25th 1895.
     his wife Eliza McGregor, Feb. 8th 1814 - April 1st 1874.
     his wife Catharine Davis, b. Dec. 8th 1818 - Sept. 29th 1871.
John Babcock died Aug. 10th 1822 AE 82 yrs.
     Mrs. Eugene M. Olmstead, 12859 West Parkway, Detroit, MI 48223, has been working on the descendants of Amy Babcock, born Alburg in 1808, daughter of Ichabod and Sarah (Pike) Babcock.

T. M. Babcock, late of Rockville, MD, identified the John Babcock of Stephentown, New York, who was mentioned in *Slade-Babcock Genealogy* as having been a Supervisor of Stephentown in 1817. He was John[6] Babcock (John[5], Ichabod[4], John[3], John[2], James[1]), who was born in Westerly, Rhode Island, 13 Jan. 1769, and was married by Elder Henry Joslin on 10 Jan. 1790 to Anna Maxson, daughter of Jonathan Maxson of Richmond, Rhode Island. Mr. Babcock's research was continued with the assistance of Mrs. Frances D. Broderick.

DEBOZEAR - The compiler of this work has in his possession a deed by Monument Cemetery, dated 14 Sept. 1839, to Lewis Debozear for lots B:658, C:338, C:339 and C:367. The latter three lots were sold to Wm. H. Moore on 22 May 1846.

EVANS - John Evans, brother of Jane[2] Evans (page 187), has been treated in *The Dictionary of Welsh Biography Down to 1940* [219]. He died 25 May 1830, aged 55, leaving a widow who died 19 Jan. 1850. A printer at Barmouth, and from 1795 at Carmarthen, he was considered a craftsman at his trade. A competitor to John Daniel, he printed the four editions of "Peter Williams' Bible." He was the founder of the Carmarthen *Journal*, a weekly newspaper which was carried on by his son David from 1820 to 18 July 1823, by his son John to 1832, and by his son William until 9 July 1844.

Children, born in Wales:

    i.   David.

    ii.   John, d. 7 Jan. 1840, aged 42.

   iii.   William, d. 1847.

FISH - Grizzel[2] (Strange) Fish was married second to Samuel Cornell.

§ § §

The following bibliography lists some representative examples, and should be studied with care with particular emphasis on the components of an entry, spacing and punctuation.

BIBLIOGRAPHY

The abbreviations used in this bibliography are explained on the last page of this section.

Aldrich, Lewis Cass, ed. *History of Franklin and Grand Isle Counties, Vermont.* Syracuse: D. Mason & Co., Publishers, 1891.

American and English Genealogies in the Library of Congress. Washington: Government Printing Office, 1919.

Anderson, George Baker. *Landmarks of Rensselaer County, New York.* D. Mason & Company, Publishers, 1897.

Anderson, Robert Charles. "Ancestry of President Calvin Coolidge," *TAG*, 53 (1977), 65ff.

Anderson, Robert V. "Geertje Nannings' Daughter and the Name Nannings," *TAG*, 54 (1978), 6-8.

Anthony, John Gould. "Genealogy of the Anthonys of New England," *NEHGR*, 31 (1877), 416-417.

Appleton, W. S. *The Badcock Family of Massachusetts.* Boston, 1881.

Appleton, W. S. "Family of Babcock of Milton, Mass.," *NEHGR*, 19 (1865), 215-219.

Arnold, Samuel Greene. *History of the State of Rhode Island and Providence Plantations*, 4th ed., 2 vols. Providence, R. I.: Preston & Rounds, 1894.

Avery, Samuel Putnam. "Avery," *NYGBR*, 51 (1920), 84-87.

Babcock, George Milton. "A Branch of the Babcock Family," *UGHM*, 5 (1914), 20-24.

Babcock, George Milton. *On the Banks of the Hudson.* Fontana, Calif., 1968.

Babcock, Stephen. *Babcock Genealogy.* New York: Eaton & Maine, 1903.

Banks, Charles Edward. *The English Ancestry and Homes of the Pilgrim Fathers.* New York: The Grafton Press, 1929.

Banks, Charles Edward. "John and Edward Tilley of the 'Mayflower,' a Correction," *NYGBR*, 60 (1929), 14.

Banks, Charles Edward. *The Planters of the Commonwealth.* Baltimore: Genealogical Publishing Co., 1961.

Banks, Charles Edward. *Topographical Dictionary of 2885 English Emigrants to New England, 1620-1650*, ed. Elijah Ellsworth Brownell. Baltimore: Southern Book Co., 1957.

Barbier, Paul fils. *The Age of Owain Gwynedd, an Attempt at a Connected Account of the History of Wales from December, 1135, to November, 1170.* London: David Nutt, 1908.

Beale, Howard K. "Theodore Roosevelt's Ancestry, a Study in Heredity," *NYGBR*, 85 (1954), 196-205 [with folding chart].

Bemis, Julia Draper (Watson), and Alonzo Amasa Bemis. *History and Genealogy of the Watson Family, Descendants of Matthew Watson, who*

Came to America in 1718. Spencer, Mass., 1894.

Benton, Rev. G. Montagu. "Wivenhoe Records," *Essex Review*, 37 (1928), 156-169.

Bergen, Teunis J. *Register of the Early Settlers of Kings County, Long Island, N. Y., from Its First Settlement by Europeans to 1700.* New York: S. W. Green's Son, 1881.

Bergman, Leola Nelson. *Americans from Norway.* Philadelphia: J. B. Lippincott Company, 1950.

Blackman, Nathan Lincoln, and Alfred L. Holman. *Blackman and Allied Families.* Chicago, 1928.

Blagg, Thomas M., and F. Arthur Wadsworth, eds. *Abstracts of Nottinghamshire Marriage Licenses*, 2 vols. London: The British Record Society, 1930-1935.

Blodgette, George Brainard. *Early Settlers of Rowley, Massachusetts.* Rowley: Amos Everett Jewett, 1933.

Bond, Thomas Edward. *Jenckes-Jenks Genealogy.* MS copy, 1952 [Los Angeles Public Library].

Boston Marriages from 1700 to 1751 [A Report of the Record Commissioners of the City of Boston, vol. 28]. Boston: Municipal Printing Office, 1898.

Bowen, Clarence Winthrop. *The History of Woodstock, Connecticut: Genealogies of Woodstock Families*, 8 vols. Worcester, Mass.: American Antiquarian Society, 1926-1943.

Broderick, Frances D. "'Honest' John Babcock of Grafton, New York," *SBGN*, 1 (1968), 3-5.

Brownson, Lydia B. (Phinney), and MacLean W. McLean. "Thomas[1] Landers of Sandwich, Mass. (ca. 1613-1675)," *NEHGR*, 124 (1970), 42ff.

Bullock, Hon. J. Russell. "Richard Bullock of Rehoboth, 1644, and Some of His Descendants," *NGSQ*, 5 (1916), 49ff.

Bunting, Morgan. "The Names of the Early Settlers of Darby Township, Chester County, Pennsylvania," *PMHB*, 24 (1900-01), 182-186.

[Chace, Oliver.] *Genealogy of the Ancestors and Descendants of Joseph Chase, Who Died in Swanzey, His Will Proved March, 1725*. Fall River, Mass., 1874.

Chamberlain, George Walter. *History of Weymouth, Massachusetts - Genealogy of Weymouth Families*, 4 vols. 1923.

Chapin, Charles V., et al. *Alphabetical Index of the Births, Marriages, and Deaths Recorded in Providence*, 25 vols. Providence, R. I., n. d.

Christensen, Gloria M. "Is Joan (Hurst) Rogers the Mother of Elizabeth Tilley?" *The Howland Quarterly*, 41 (Jan.-April 1977), 3-4.

"The Clarendon Papers," *Collections of the New-York Historical Society for the Year 1869*. New York, 1870.

Colket, Meredith B. Jr. "Memorandum Concerning John Jenks of London." MS, [1968] [with letter to compiler dated 1 Nov. 1968].

Collins, Thomas E. Manuscript Notes. [Ventura, California].

Committee on Genealogy of the First Congregational Church of Dighton, Massachusetts. *1708-1958; Dighton; Past and Present*. 1958.

Cooke, Robert, Clarenceux King of Arms. *Visitation of London in the Year 1568*. London: Harleian Society, 1869.

Cooke, Robert, Clarenceux King of Arms. *Visitation of London, 1568*, ed. H. Stanford London. London: Harleian Society, 1963.

Connett, Mrs. Myron. "Salisbury Bible Records," *The Searcher*, 5 (1968), 66-67.

Davis, William T. *Ancient Landmarks of Plymouth*, 2nd ed. Boston: Damrell & Upham, 1899.

Eck, Aimee [May] (Huston). *John Browne, Gentleman of Wannamoisett*. Minneapolis, 1951.

Ewers, Dorothy Wood. *Descendants of John Wood, a Mariner, Who Died in Portsmouth, Rhode Island in 1665.* Ann Arbor: University Microfilms International, 1978.

"Falmouth, Mass., Records," *The Genealogical Advertizer,* 3 (1900), 57ff.

Fuller, Carol Seager. *An Incident at Hartford.* Brevard, N. C.: Cordelia T. Seager & Charles W. Seager, 1979.

Gover, J. E. B., Allen Mawer, and F. M. Stanton. *The Place Names of Hertfordshire.* Cambridge: University Press [English Place-Name Society, vol. 15], 1938.

MD   - *Mayflower Descendant*
NEHGR - *The New England Historical and Genealogical Register*
NGSQ   - *National Genealogical Society Quarterly*
NYGBR - *The New York Genealogical and Biographical Magazine*
PMHB   - *The Pennsylvania Magazine of History and Biography*
RIGR   - *Rhode Island Genealogical Register*
SBGN   - *The Slade-Babcock Genealogical Newsletter*
TAG   - *The American Genealogist*
UGHM   - *The Utah Genealogical and Historical Magazine*

§ § §

Note: As stated in the text, each entry for a book must contain the author or authors, the title, the place of publication (if given), the name of the publisher (if given) and the date of publication (if given). Occasionally it is necessary to list a book by author and title followed by "N. p., n. d." This means that no place, publisher or date is given. However, it is usually possible to discover some of this information, in which case it can be printed in brackets.

Examples are given above for manuscripts, the abbreviation MS being appropriate (see the Colket entry).

Periodical articles must include, insofar as the information exists, the author, title of article (in quotation marks), title of periodical (in italics or underlined), volume number, year of publication (the date being necessary if each issue begins with page 1), and the page numbers. For an article continued over a number of pages or issues, use the first page number with "ff." for "following."

INDEXING

You cannot please everyone with your index format. Some people want all items indexed alphabetically, including ships, place names, personal names and authors. I have indexed ship names first, then place names subdivided according to country and state, and all personal names, including those of authors or compilers of references. The indexing of authors may be of help to reviewers.

Then questions arise as to whether you should use a two column or three column format. Generally this is dictated by considerations of space. For some material the two column format is more efficient.

§ § §

GENEALOGICAL BOOK STORES

Book stores do not generally prove to be good customers for genealogies and family histories. Several dozen dealers in the United States do carry a selection of manuals, reference works, forms and the like, but they do not stock genealogies due to the large number of titles and the small demand for each one.

Two shops, however, do publish genealogical catalogs for sale, and may list your work if you contact them about your book, offering a 40% discount. They are:

Goodspeed's Book Shop, 7 Beacon Street, Boston, MA 02108
Tuttle Antiquarian Books, P. O. Box 541, Rutland, VT 05701

As the catalogs are not published frequently, it may be some time before your title is listed. However, the listing does generally result in some sales. The store will order on demand, and should be advised when the supply is getting short.

§ § §

GENEALOGICAL SOCIETIES AND LIBRARIES

The most recent edition of *The Handy Guide for Genealogists* will list societies and libraries, many of which may purchase genealogies of particular interest. This list is updated annually in *The Genealogical Helper*. The lists do contains duplications and error which will be apparent to the careful reader.

Those listed below have ordered several titles from this publisher directly, including genealogies.

Acquisitions Department, Springfield City Library, 220 State Street, Springfield, MA 01103

The Berkshire Athenaeum, 1 Wendell Avenue, Pittsfield, MA 01201

The American Antiquarian Society Library, 185 Salisbury Street, Worcester, MA 01609

Old Colony Historical Society, 66 Church Green, Taunton, MA 02780

The Rhode Island Historical Society Library, 121 Hope Street, Providence, RI 02906

Acquisitions Supervisor, New Hampshire State Library, 20 Park Street, Concord, NH 03301

Maine State Library, Augusta, ME 04333

Connecticut Historical Society, 1 Elizabeth Street, Hartford, CT 06105

Mrs. E.P. Whitten, Asst. Dir., The Public Library of New London, 63 Huntington Street, New London, CT 06320

Godfrey Memorial Library, 134 Newfield Street, Middletown, CT 06457

New Haven Colony Historical Society, 114 Whitney Avenue, New Haven, CT 06510

Westfield Memorial Library, 425 East Broad Street, Westfield, NJ 07090

New Jersey Historical Society, 230 Broadway, Newark, NJ 07104

Joint Free Library of Morristown and Morris Township, 1 Miller Road, Box 267 M, Morristown, NJ 07960

Morris County Free Library, 30 East Hanover Avenue, Whippany, NJ 07981

Savitz Library Special Collections, Glassboro State College, Glassboro, NJ 08028

Vineland Historical and Antiquarian Society, 108 South Seventh Street, Vineland, NJ 08360

New Jersey State Library, Acquisitions Section, 185 West State Street, Trenton, NJ 08625-0520

Acquisition Division, New York Public Library, Fifth Avenue and 42nd Street, New York, NY 10018

Huntington Public Library, 338 Main Street, Huntington, NY 11743

New York State Library, Monographic Control Section, Cultural Educ. Center, 6th Floor, Albany, NY 12224

Newburgh Free Library, 124 Grand Street, Newburgh, NY 12550

Onondaga County Public Library, Local History and Genealogy Department, 335 Montgomery Street, Syracuse, NY 13202

State Library of Pennsylvania, J.B. Newman, Genealogy and Local History, P.O. Box 1601, Harrisburg, PA 17105

Historical Society of Pennsylvania, 1300 Locust Street, Philadelphia, PA 19107

Enoch Pratt Free Library, 400 Cathedral Street, Baltimore, MD 21201

Library Acquisitions, Maryland Historical Society, 201 West Monument Street, Baltimore, MD 21201

Maryland State Library, Court of Appeals Building, 361 Rose Boulevard, Annapolis, MD 21401

Fairfax County Public Library, 5502 Port Royal Road, Springfield, VA 22151

Order Section, Virginia State Library, 1101 Capitol, Richmond, VA 23219

City of Roanoke, Roanoke Public Library, 706 South Jefferson Street, Roanoke, VA 24011

Public Library of Charlotte and Mecklenburg Counties, 310 North Tyron Street, Charlotte, NC 28202

Robeson County Public Library, 101 North Chestnut Street, Box 1346, Lumberton, NC 28358

Transylvania County Library, 105 South Broad Street, Brevard, NC 28712

South Carolina State Library, P.O. Box 11469, Columbia, SC 29211

Charleston County Library, 404 King Street, Charleston, SC 29403

Greenville County Library, 300 College Street, Greenville, SC 29601

Atlanta-Fulton Public Library, 1 Margaret Mitchell Square, N.W., Carnegie Way at Forsyth Street, Atlanta, GA 30303

Georgia Department of Archives and History, 330 Capitol Avenue, Atlanta, GA 30334

Jacksonville Public Library, 122 North Ocean Street, Jacksonville, FL 32202

Acquisitions Section, State Library of Florida, R.A. Gray Building, Tallahassee, FL 32304

Orlando Public Library, 10 North Rosalind Avenue, Orlando, FL 32801

Tampa-Hillsborough County Public Library System, 900 North Ashley Street, Tampa, FL 33602

Department of Archives and History, 624 Washington Avenue, Montgomery, AL 36130

Liles Memorial Library, 108 East Tenth Street, Box 308, Anniston, AL 36201

Chattanooga-Hamilton County Bicentennial Library, 1001 Broad Street, Chattanooga, TN 37402

Blount County Library, 301 McGhee Street, Maryville, TN 37801

Memphis Public Library and Information Center, 1850 Peabody, Memphis, TN 38104

Jackson-Madison County Library, 433 East Lafayette, Jackson, TN 38301

Mississippi Department of Archives and History, P.O. Box 571, Jackson, MS 39205

Lincoln-Lawrence-Franklin Regional Library, P.O. Box 541, Brookhaven, MS 39601

Filson Club Library, 118 West Breckenridge Street, Louisville, KY 40203

Library, Kentucky Historical Society, Old Capitol Annex, Box H, Frankfort, KY 40602

Ohio Historical Society Library, I-17 and 17th Avenue, Columbus, Ohio 43211

Technical Services, The State Library of Ohio, 65 South Front Street, Columbus, OH 43215

The Library, The Western Reserve Historical Society, 10825 East Boulevard, Cleveland, OH 44106

Cuyahoga County Public Library, 4510 Memphis Avenue, Cleveland, OH 44144

The Public Library of Cincinnati and Hamilton County, 800 Vine Street, Cincinnati, OH 45202

Amos Memorial Public Library, 230 East North Street, Sidney, OH 45365

Noblesville Public Library, 16 South Tenth Street, Noblesville, IN 46060

Genealogy Division, Indiana State Library, 140 North Senate Avenue, Indianapolis, IN 46204

Lake County Public Library, 1919 West Lincoln Highway, Merrillville, IN 46410-5382

The Allen County Public Library, P.O. Box 2270, Fort Wayne, IN 46801

Acquisitions, Monroe County Public Library, 303 East Kirkwood Avenue, Bloomington, IN 47401

Monroe County Library System, 3700 South Custer Road, Monroe, MI 48161

Burton Historical Collection, Detroit Public Library, 5201 Woodward Avenue, Detroit, MI 48202

Capital Library Cooperative, 407 North Cedar Street, Mason, MI 48854

Michigan Department of Education, State Library Service, Box 30007, Lansing, MI 48909

Ames Public Library, 210 Sixth Street, Ames, IA 50010

State Historical Society of Iowa Library, 402 Iowa Avenue, Iowa City, IA 52240

Milwaukee Public Library, 814 West Wisconsin Avenue, Milwaukee, WI 53233

State Historical Society of Wisconsin, 816 State Street, Madison, WI 53706

Acquisitions/EDP Department, Minneapolis Public Library, 300 Nicolet Avenue, Minneapolis, MN 55401

Arlington Heights Memorial Library, 500 North Dunton Avenue, Arlington Heights, IL 60004

Zion Benton Public Library, 2400 Gabriel Avenue, Zion, IL 60099

Lyons Public Library, 4209 Joliet Avenue, Lyons, IL 60534

Order Department, Newberry Library, 60 West Walton Street, Chicago, IL 60610

Shawnee Library System, Rural Route 2, Box 136A, Carterville, IL 62918

St. Louis Public Library, 1301 Olive Street, St. Louis, MO 63103

Kansas State Historical Society, 120 West Tenth, Topeka, KS 66612

Independence Public Library, 220 East Maple, Independence, KS 67301

South Central Kansas Library System, Mrs. Donna Whitson, 901 North Main Street, Hutchinson, KS 67501

Southwest Nebraska Genealogical Society, Box 6, McCook, NE 69001

Acquisition Division, New Orleans Public Library, 219 Loyola Avenue, New Orleans, LA 70140

St. Martin Parish Library, 105 South New Market Street, St. Martinville, LA 70582

Louisiana State Library, Readers' Services, P.O. Box 131, Baton Rouge, LA 70821

Shreve Memorial Library, Genealogy Department, P.O. Box 21523, Shreveport, LA 71120

The Public Library of Camden and Ouachita County, 120 Harrison Avenue, S.W., Camden, AR 71701

Central Arkansas Library System, 700 Louisiana Street, Little Rock, AR 72201

Genealogical Society of Van Zandt County, P.O. Box 434, Wills Point, TX 75169

Order Division, Fort Worth Public Library, 300 Taylor Street, Fort Worth, TX 76102

Waco-McLennan County Library, 1717 Austin Avenue, Waco, TX 76701

Houston Public Library, Acquisitions Department, 500 McKinney Street, Houston, TX 77002

Texas State Library, Technical Services, Box 12927, Capitol Station, Austin, TX 78711

County Library, P.O. Box 1191, Midland, TX 79702

El Paso Public Library, Document Genealogy Department, 501 North Oregon Street, El Paso, TX 79901

Acquisitions Department, Denver Public Library, 3840 I York Street, Denver, CO 80205-3536

Genealogy Department, Laramie County Public Library, 2800 Central Avenue, Cheyanne, WY 82001

Mormon Pioneer Genealogical Society, Michel L. Call, P.O. Box 11488, Salt Lake City, UT 84147

Acquisitions, Genealogical Library, 35 North West Temple Street, Salt Lake City, UT 84150

Order Department, 6382 HBLL, Brigham Young University, Provo, UT 84602

Acquisitions Department, Albuquerque Public Library, 501 Copper N.W., Albuquerque, NM 87102

Sons of the Revolution, 600 South Central Avenue, Glendale, CA 91209

Southern California Genealogical Society, P.O. Box 4377, Burbank, CA 91503

San Diego Regional Genealogical Society, 3705 Tenth Avenue, San Diego, CA 92103

San Diego Genealogical Society, 3030 Kellogg Street, San Diego, CA 92106

Family History Center, San Bernardino Stake #173, P.O. Box 432, San Bernardino, CA 92403

Orange County Genealogical Society, P.O. Box 1587, Orange, CA 92668

Kern County Library, 1315 Truxton Avenue, Bakersfield, CA 93301

Monterey Bay Family History Center, P.O. Box 7278, Spreckels, CA 93962

California State Library, Sutro Branch, 480 Winston Drive, San Francisco, CA 94132

Eureka Family History Center, 2734 Dolbeer Street, Eureka, CA 95501

Sacramento Family History Center, 5343 Halstead Avenue, Carmichael, CA 95608

Acquisitions Section, California State Library, Sacramento, CA 95809

Library Association of Portland and Multnomah County, 801 S.W. Tenth Avenue, Portland, OR 97205

Library Division, Portland Community College, 12000 S.W. 49th Avenue, Portland, OR 97219

Oregon State Library, State Library Building, Summer and Court Streets, Salem, OR 97310

Cottage Grove Genealogical Society, W.A. Woodard Memorial Library, Sixth and Washington Streets, Cottage Grove, OR 97424

Order Unit, Seattle Public Library, 1000 Fourth Avenue, Seattle, WA 98104

Order Department, Metropolitan Toronto Library, 789 Yonge Street, Toronto, Ontario, Canada M4W 2G8

USING WORDPERFECT 5.0 TO PROCESS GENEALOGY

It took some weeks, and much trial and error, to learn to do the word processing for genealogical materials. While there is a useful book in print on the subject, it does not show how to justify the text neatly; thus the need for this appendix.

The following example illustrates the processing used in the forthcoming *Ancestral Lines, Third Edition*. Explanatory material is given in Swiss Roman type, commands are given in **Dutch Roman bold type**, and the text is presented in regular Dutch Roman type.

The first step is to set up and save a basic format which can be pulled up from disc at your convenience. First type [**Shift+F8**(format)]. This means that while holding down the Shift key, press the F8 key to begin the format. Then type [**1**(line)][**7**(margins)]**1.6"[Enter]1.6"[Enter]**. You have set the left and right margins. To set the tabs continue by typing [**8**(tab set)]**1.8"**[arrow right (to 2.0")]**D**(to change the "L" regular tab to a decimal tab)**2.4"[Enter]D[arrow right** (to 2.5")][**Delete**]**2.6"[Enter] 2.8"[Enter]3.2"[Enter][F7** (exit)]. This completes setting the tabs, including two decimal tabs. Watch the screen closely while later typing the material on the children and you will see how the decimal tabs work.

Continue typing [**9**][**Y**][**0**][**2**][**5**]**1.08"[Enter]1.08"[Enter][8][1][1][0][0] [Control**(or Ctrl)**+F8**][**4**(base font)][arrow (up or down as needed)][**1** (select)][**F10**(save)]**b:\format.bsc[Enter]**. Now you have saved your basic format to your "b" drive. You can bring this to the screen any time you wish to type additional genealogy. Just make sure that you go to the end of the format before typing your material.

Now we will turn to how to process the following entry. Notice it contains small letters above the line, small upper case letters, italics, a variety of indentations, a foreign symbol (the British pound sign), super-numerals, and a special closing symbol.

ABELL

There were several branches of the Abell family in Derbyshire, England, by the sixteenth century. The brothers John and Richard Abell were the progenitors of the branch at Creighton and Uttoxeter. Richard died before 1536. Henry Abell, who died in 1540, was the earliest known member of the Sommersall branch. Nicholas Abell, the first known member of the Norbury branch, died about 1557. The fourth branch of the family, at Stapenhill, was descended from Robert[C] Abell, below [Abell].

The sources have been rechecked and confirmed by Gary Boyd Roberts and others.

1. ROBERT[C] ABELL, Esquire, of Stapenhill, Derbyshire, England, was of record there about 1533-1538, in a complaint brought by one Walter Blount [see *Chancery Proc. Early 725/38, 738/10*], and in a deed dated 1547.

A Robert Abell, gentleman, was a servant or tenant to Sir William Gryseley and was at Bryslincote, Derbyshire, in 9 Henry VIII (1517-1518) [see *Star Chamber Proc. 19/159*].

Children, listed from family wills:

    i. Anthony, d. 1559; m. (1) Elizabeth, m. (2) Elizabeth; of Ticknall, Derbyshire, gent.

    ii. George, d. 1597 [*P.C.C. Cobham 43*]; m. Helene; of Newborough, Staffordshire, and Stapenhill.

2.   iii. Robert, d. 1588; m.

    iv. daughter, m. Royle.

    v. Anne, d. 1577; unm.

2. ROBERT[B] ABELL, of Stapenhill and Ticknall, Derbyshire, England, left a will, dated 18 March 1587/8, which was proved in London 17 May 1588 [*P.C.C. Rutland 33*] by Edward Orwell, notary public.

His wife, not mentioned in his will, apparently died before him.

Child, only one mentioned in will:

3.   i. George, d. 1631; m. Frances[A] Cotton.

3. GEORGE[A] ABELL, born about 1561, was buried in Lockington, Leicestershire, England, 13 Sept. 1630.

He married FRANCES[A] COTTON*, who was living in 1630.

Of Stapenhill, Derbyshire, and Hemington in the parish of Lockington, he matriculated at Brasenose College, Oxford, 8 Dec. 1578, aged 17, and was admitted to the Inner Temple in 1581. He inherited "all the tithes of Ticknall" belonging to his father in 1588. His will, dated 8 Sept. 1630 and proved 7 Feb. 1631 [*P.C.C. St. John 10*], named "my brother Andrew Cotten of Cumbermeer in ye Countie of Chester gent" to invest a bequest of £10 for the benefit of Richard Abell, the third son who was still an apprentice. Andrew Cotton was also named sole executor of the will, with authority to dispose of the residue of the estate for the benefit of George Abell's widow and eldest son "with ye advise of my brother George Cotton of Cumbermere aforesaid esquier" [Thompson, *TG*, 5:160].

Another item in his will read, "I bequeath unto my second sonne Robert Abell onelie a Twentie shillings peece for his childs parte in regard of ye charges I have beene at in placeing him in a good trade in London wch hee hath made noe use of and since in furnishing him for newe England where I hope he now is."

Thompson [*Ibid.*] has built a substantial case for the identification of George Abell's wife Frances Cotton, discussing the known relationships and concluding, "the only possible brotherly relationship between George Abell and George and Andrew Cotton of Combermere must arise from the marriage of their sister Frances to George Abell from Hemington. Moreover, Frances (Cotton) Abell must have been the mother of the children, for otherwise her brothers would have had no particular enthusiasm for the protection of their financial interests."

Children, born in England:

      i. George, eldest son; perhaps later in Connecticut.

4.   ii. Robert[1], d. Rehoboth, Plymouth Colony, 20 June 1663; m. Joannah.

     iii. Richard, third son.

     iv. Mary, received bequests from her aunt Dorothy Cotton, spinster, by will dated 16 April 1646.

4. ROBERT[1] ABELL, born in England, perhaps in Hemington, Leicestershire, probably after 1600, died in Rehoboth, Plymouth Colony, 20 June 1663.

He married, possibly in England [Abell, 43], but more likely in Weymouth, Massachusetts Bay, JOANNAH, who married second, in 1667, William[1] Hyde, and died in Norwich, Connecticut, after 1682.

According to his father's will, Robert Abell had been placed "in a good trade in London wch hee hath made noe use of." His father then furnished him for New England, and it is probable he came to America with Governor Winthrop's fleet, arriving at Charlestown, Mass. Bay, in June 1630. He was included in the list of those desiring to be made freemen at Weymouth 19 Oct. 1630, and on 18 May 1631 he took the oath of freeman there.

He name was mentioned occasionally in the records of the Quarterly Courts at Boston and Weymouth, and although he was not among the original proprietors of Rehoboth in the meetings at Weymouth as early as 24 Oct. 1643, he apparently purchased Job Lane's share before the settlement was made. He was among those who drew lots for lands in the new meadow 18 Feb. 1646, and on 26 Feb. 1651/2 he and Richard Bullock (q.v.) were chosen to burn the commons and be paid 20/- out of the first rate. On 1 Feb. 1654 he was ordered to keep the Ordinary, or restaurant, in Rehoboth, and he was a member of the jury at the General Court in Plymouth 3 June 1657. His name, and the names of his heirs, has been found on lists of lot drawings in 1658 and 1668. The inventory of his estate, taken 9 August 1663, totaled £354.17s.9d, of which £130 was the value of his home and land. His widow was administratrix of his estate.

Through their son Caleb they were ancestors of President Grover Cleveland [G.B. Roberts' *Ancestors of American Presidents*, 40-43].

Children, of record at Weymouth, Rehoboth and Norwich:

   i.   Abraham[2], d. Weymouth, Mass., 14 Nov. 1639.
 * ii.   Mary, b. Weymouth 11 April 1642; m. Samuel[2] Luther.
  iii.   Preserved, b. Rehoboth 1644; d. there 18 August 1724; m. (1) 27 Sept. 1667 Martha Redaway, m. (2) 27 Dec. 1686 Sarah[2] Bowen, m. (3) int. Rehoboth 30 Dec. 1706 Mrs. Anne West of Boston.
   iv.   Caleb, b. 1646; d. Norwich, Conn., 7 August 1731, in 85th year; m. (1) Norwich July 1669 Margaret Post, m. (2) 25 June 1701 Mary Miller.
    v.   Joshua, b. 1649; d. 1 March 1725, bur. Norwich; m. (1) 1 Nov. 167- Mehitobell Smith, m. (2) Nov. 1685 Bethiah[3] Gager.
   vi.   Benjamin, d. Norwich 1699; m. c. 1678 Hannah (?Baldwin), who m. (2) David Caulkins, Sr.
  vii.   Experience, d. after 5 June 1705; m. Guilford, Conn., 1680, John Baldwin.
 viii.   child, name unknown, mentioned in father's will, which enumerated oldest son, dau. Mary and five others.

§ § §

Now that you have read the entry it is time to turn to the processing steps. First, bring up from your "b" drive your basic format by typing your list key, which is F5, and entering b:\format.bsc. The format brought up will control margins, spacing, tabs and font.

Now type [**Shift+F6**(center)]ABELL[**Enter**][**Enter**][**Tab**]There were several branches of the Abell family in Derbyshire, England, by the sixteenth century. The brothers John and Richard Abell were the progenitors of the branch at Creighton and Uttoxeter. Richard died before 1536. Henry Abell, who died in 1540, was the earliest known member of the Sommersall branch. Nicholas Abell, the first known member of the Norbury branch, died about 1557. The fourth branch of the family, at Stapenhill, was descended from RobertC[**arrow left** once][**F12**][**arrow right** once][**Control+F8**][**1**][**1**][This turns the C in RobertC into a ᶜ] Abell, below [Abell].[**Enter**]

[**Tab**]The sources have been rechecked and confirmed by Gary Boyd Roberts and others.[**Enter**]

[**Enter**]

[**Tab**]1.   ROBERT[**arrow left** to O in R<u>O</u>BERT][**F12** *or* **Alt+F4** (to block)][**arrow right** to space right of T in ROBER<u>T</u> so that OBERT is all highlighted][**1**][**4**][This makes it look like Rᴏʙᴇʀᴛ]C[**arrow left** once][**F12**][**arrow right** once][**Control+F8**][**1**][**1**][This again turns the C in ROBERTC into a ᶜ] ABELL[**arrow left** to B in A<u>B</u>ELL][**F12** *or* **Alt+F4** (to block) and then **arrow right** to space right of second L in ABEL<u>L</u> so that BELL is all highlighted][**1**][**4**][This makes it look like Aʙᴇʟʟ], Esquire, of Stapenhill, Derbyshire, England, was of record there about 1533-1538, in a complaint brought by one Walter Blount [see Chancery Proc. Early 725/38, 738/10[**arrow left** to C in <u>C</u>hancery][**F12** (to begin block)][**arrow right** to] in 738/10]][**Control+F8**][**2**][**4**][this will make it appear to be like [see *Chancery Proc. Early 725/38, 738/10*]]], and in a deed dated 1547.[**Enter**]

[**Tab**]A Robert Abell, gentleman, was a servant or tenant to Sir William Gryseley and was at Bryslincote, Derbyshire, in 9 Henry VIII (1517-1518) [see Star Chamber Proc. 19/159[**arrow left** to S in <u>S</u>tar][**F12** (to begin block)][**arrow right** to] in 19/159] to put into italics *Star Chamber Proc. 19/159*][**2**][**4**].[**Enter**]

[**Tab**]Children, listed from family wills:[**Enter**]

[**Tab**][**Tab**][**Tab**]i.[**Tab**]Anthony, d. 1559; m. (1) Elizabeth, m. (2) Elizabeth; of Ticknall,[**arrow left** to margin and then strike [**Tab**] five times] Derbyshire, gent.[**Enter**]

[**Tab**][**Tab**][**Tab**]ii.[**Tab**]George, d. 1597 [P.C.C. Cobham 43[**arrow left** to P.C.C.][**F12**][**arrow right** to space right of 43][**2**][**4**]; m. Helene; of Newborough[**arrow left** to b in New<u>b</u>orough][**Control+-(hyphen)**][**arrow up**][**arrow down** (this shows how the word is hyphenated)][**arrow left** to margin and then strike [**Tab**] five times], Staffordshire, and Stapenhill.[**Enter**]

[**Tab**][**Tab**]2.[**Tab**]iii.[**Tab**]Robert, d. 1588; m.[**Enter**]

[**Tab**][**Tab**][**Tab**]iv.[**Tab**]daughter, m. Royle.[**Enter**]

[**Tab**][**Tab**][**Tab**]v.[**Tab**]Anne, d. 1577; unm.[**Enter**]

[**Enter**]

[**Tab**]2.   ROBERT[**arrow left** to O in R<u>O</u>BERT][**F12** (to block, **Alt+F4** can also be used if you have only ten function keys on your computer][**arrow right** to space right of T in ROBER<u>T</u> so that OBERT is all highlighted][**1**][**4**]B[**arrow left** once][**Control+F8**][**1**][**1**] ABELL, of

Stapenhill and Ticknall, Derbyshire, England, left a will, dated 18 March 1587/8, which was proved in London 17 May 1588 [P.C.C. Rutland 33[arrow left to first letter of area to be italicized][F12][arrow right to highlight entire area to be italicized][2][4]] by Edward Orwell, notary public.[Enter]
[Tab]His wife, not mentioned in his will, apparently died before him.[Enter]
[Tab]Child, only one mentioned in will:[Enter]
[Tab][Tab]3.[Tab]i.[Tab]George, d. 1631; m. FrancesA[highlight the letter A to be superscripted, using the block function, and type [1][1]] Cotton.[Enter]
[Enter]
[Tab]3. GEORGE[arrow left to E in GEORGE][F12][arrow right to highlight area to be put in small upper case letters][Control+F8][1][4] A [arrow left once] [F12] [arrow right once] [Control+F8] [1] [1] ABELL[block the area to be changed in to small upper case letters and use Control+F8 and [1][4]], born about 1561, was buried in Lockington, Leicestershire [remember that words which need to be hyphenated can be marked with a Control+-], England, 13 Sept. 1630.[Enter]
[Tab]He married FRANCES[block and convert appropriate letters to small upper case]A[change to superscript using Control+F8 and [1][1] on blocked letter A] COTTON[change OTTON to small upper case]*, who was living in 1630.[Enter]
[Tab]Of Stapenhill, Derbyshire, and Hemington in the parish of Lockington, he matriculated at Brasenose College, Oxford, 8 Dec. 1578, aged 17, and was admitted to the Inner Temple in 1581. He inherited "all the tithes of Ticknall" belonging to his father in 1588. His will, dated 8 Sept. 1630 and proved 7 Feb. 1631 [P.C.C. St. John 10[change the P.C.C. St. John 10 to *italics* by blocking it and then using Control+F8 and [2][4]], named "my brother Andrew Cotten of Cumbermeer in ye Countie of Chester gent" to invest a bequest of [Control+v]4,11[Enter]10 [notice how the Control+v function is used to bring up special characters] for the benefit of Richard Abell, the third son who was still an apprentice. Andrew Cotton was also named sole executor of the will, with authority to dispose of the residue of the estate for the benefit of George Abell's widow and eldest son "with ye advise of my brother George Cotton of Cumbermere aforesaid esquier" [Thompson, TG [block TG and *italicize* using Control+F8 plus [2][4]], 5:160].[Enter]
[Tab]Another item in his will read, "I bequeath unto my second sonne Robert Abell onelie a Twentie shillings peece for his childs parte in regard of ye charges I have beene at in placeing him in a good trade in

London w^{ch} [block ch and [Control+F8][1][1]] hee hath made noe use of and since in furnishing him for newe England where I hope he now is."[Enter]

[Tab]Thompson [*Ibid.*] [do not forget to italicize] has built a substantial case for the identification of George Abell's wife Frances Cotton, discussing the known relationships and concluding, "the only possible brotherly relationship between George Abell and George and Andrew Cotton of Combermere must arise from the marriage of their sister Frances to George Abell from Hemington. Moreover, Frances (Cotton) Abell must have been the mother of the children, for otherwise her brothers would have had no particular enthusiasm for the protection of their financial interests."[Enter]

[Tab]Children, born in England:[Enter]

[Tab][Tab][Tab]i.[Tab]George, eldest son; perhaps later in Connecticut.[Enter]

[Tab][Tab]4.[Tab]ii.[Tab]Robert¹[superscript by blocking and using Control+F8 with [1][1]], d. Rehoboth, Plymouth Colony, 20 June 1663; m. Joannah.[arrow left to margin, hit Tab five times to indent properly, then arrow right to end of line][Enter]

[Tab][Tab][Tab]iii.[Tab]Richard, third son.[Enter]

[Tab][Tab][Tab]iv.[Tab]Mary, received bequests from her aunt Dorothy Cotton, spinster, by will dated 16 April 1646.[arrow left to margin, Tab fives times, then arrow right to end of line and type [Enter]]
[Enter]

[Tab]4. ROBERT¹ ABELL[using the block F12 key and Control+F8 and the screen prompts change appropriate letters to small upper case and superscript], born in England, perhaps in Hemington, Leicestershire, probably after 1600, died in Rehoboth, Plymouth Colony, 20 June 1663.

He married,[did you Enter and Tab at the paragraph?] possibly in England [Abell, 43], but more likely in Weymouth, Massachusetts Bay, JOANNAH[small upper case], who married second, in 1667, William¹ [superscript the number] Hyde, and died in Norwich, Connecticut, after 1682.

According to his father's will, Robert Abell had been placed "in a good trade in London w^{ch}[block and superscript] hee hath made noe use of." His father then furnished him for New England, and it is probable he came to America with Governor Winthrop's fleet, arriving at Charlestown, Mass. Bay, in June 1630. He was included in the list of those desiring to be made freemen at Weymouth 19 Oct. 1630, and on 18 May 1631 he took the oath of freeman there.

He name was mentioned occasionally in the records of the Quarterly Courts at Boston and Weymouth, and although he was not among the original proprietors of Rehoboth in the meetings at Weymouth as early as 24 Oct. 1643, he apparently purchased Job Lane's share before the settlement was made. He was among those who drew lots for lands in the new meadow 18 Feb. 1646, and on 26 Feb. 1651/2 he and Richard Bullock (q.v.) were chosen to burn the commons and be paid 20/- out of the first rate. On 1 Feb. 1654 he was ordered to keep the Ordinary, or restaurant, in Rehoboth, and he was a member of the jury at the General Court in Plymouth 3 June 1657. His name, and the names of his heirs, has been found on lists of lot drawings in 1658 and 1668. The inventory of his estate, taken 9 August 1663, totaled £[remember this was **Control+v** and **4,11** followed by [**Enter**]; if it does not work you need a better font]354.17s.9d, of which £[how entered?]130 was the value of his home and land. His widow was administratrix of his estate.

Through their son Caleb they were ancestors of President Grover Cleveland [G.B. Roberts' *Ancestors of American Presidents*, 40-43].

Children, of record at Weymouth, Rehoboth and Norwich:

    i.   Abraham², d. Weymouth, Mass., 14 Nov. 1639.

*   ii.   Mary, b. Weymouth 11 April 1642; m. Samuel² Luther.

[The previous line involves the problem of putting the asterisk on the page lined up exactly with the number. The way to do this is to type "*." and then, with the reveal codes function on, for which you must type **F11**, insert a blank space in place of the period. This will keep the asterisk lined up properly on the decimal tab.]

    iii.   Preserved, b. Rehoboth 1644; d. there 18 August 1724; m. (1) 27 Sept. 1667 Martha Redaway, m. (2) 27 Dec. 1686 Sarah² Bowen, m. (3) int. Rehoboth 30 Dec. 1706 Mrs. Anne West of Boston.

    iv.   Caleb, b. 1646; d. Norwich, Conn., 7 August 1731, in 85th year; m. (1) Norwich July 1669 Margaret Post, m. (2) 25 June 1701 Mary Miller.

    v.   Joshua, b. 1649; d. 1 March 1725, bur. Norwich; m. (1) 1 Nov. 167- Mehitobell Smith, m. (2) Nov. 1685 Bethiah³ Gager.

    vi.   Benjamin, d. Norwich 1699; m. c. 1678 Hannah (?Baldwin), who m. (2) David Caulkins, Sr.

    vii.   Experience, d. after 5 June 1705; m. Guilford, Conn., 1680, John Baldwin.

    viii.   child, name unknown, mentioned in father's will, which enumerated oldest son, dau. Mary and five others.

[To enter the final line of symbols type [**Control+v**]4,6[**Enter**][space bar twice][**Control+v**]4.6[**Enter**][space bar twice][**Control+v**][**Enter**]

[Enter][arrow up][Shift+F6]. If you have material following you will want to type [Enter] twice more.

§ § §

If all this seems impossibly complicated, I hope you will take comfort in the fact that I shared your feeling when I first began to use WordPerfect®. However, you are likely to find that using these steps comes almost automatically within a few hours of processing, and the results are clearly worth it.

One of the other problems I faced was the occasional need to use accent marks or letter forms never used in English. WordPerfect® 5.1, used with a not-too-sophisticated 286 computer and the HP LaserJet IIP, will form graphically any character not resident in the font you are using. None of the fonts on the market, to my knowledge, contain all of the accent marks and letter forms which can be made graphically to complete the WordPerfect® character set. You will not run into this problem as long as your genealogy is confined to common Western European languages. However, once you begin to use Polish and other Eastern European names in their original form you may wish to have this graphics capability. The alternative is to purchase new fonts.

Are you ready for a review? Establish your format:
[Shift+F7][1][7]1.6"[Enter]1.6"[Enter][8] establishes line margins and prepares for the entry of the tab set. 1.9"[arrow right to 2.0")][delete] 2.1"[Enter]D(to make this tab a decimal tab)[arrow right to 2.5"]D[arrow right]2.7"[Enter][arrow right]2.9"[Enter][arrow right to 3.0"][delete]3.1" [Enter]3.3"[Enter][F7(exit)][9(to turn on Widows/ophans protection)]Y[0] [2][5(to start margins top and bottom)]1.08"[Enter]1.08"[Enter][8(paper size)][1(standard)][1][0][0][Control+F8][4(to choose base font)][arrow as needed][1(select)][F10]b:\basic.fmt[Enter].
[Shift+F6(center)]ARMINGTON[Enter][Enter]
[Tab]Further searches in the records of Guernsey and Boston, Massachusetts[arrow left to c in Massachusetts][Control+-][arrow up and arrow down to check how the hyphen took], are necessary to establish a better record of the immigrant ancestor. A check of the indices of selected volumes of the *Record Commissioner Reports for Boston* revealed nothing of the name.[Enter]
[Enter]
[Tab]1. JOSEPH[1] ARMINGTON [arrow left to O in JOSEPH1][F12] [arrow right to 1 in JOSEPH1 to highlight or block OSEPH][Control+F8] [1][4][arrow right to R in ARMINGTON][F12][arrow right to highlight

RMINGTON][**Control+F8**][**1**][**4**][**arrow left** to 1 in JOSEPH1][**arrow right** once to highlight only the digit][**1**][**1**], born on the island of Guernsey in the English Channel, now part of the States of Jersey, perhaps about 1680, was reputed to have died in England about 1715.[**Enter**]

[**Tab**]The name of his wife was not given in the sources available to the compiler, but it was said that she was well educated and that after his death she established a school in Roxbury, Massachusetts, where she taught French.[**Enter**]

[**Tab**]Apparently they came to Boston in 1714, but he soon returned to England, dying there the next year ["Wood and Allied Families," *Americana*[**arrow left** to A in Americana][**F12**][**arrow right** to highlight Americana][**Control+F8**][**2**(appearance)][**4**(italics)], 14:169].[**Enter**]

[**Tab**]Children:[**Enter**]

[**Tab**][**Tab**][**Tab**]i.[**Tab**]Rachel2[**arrow left** to 2 in Rachel2][**F12**][**arrow right** once to highlight 2][**Control+F8**][**1**][**1**], m. Boston 11 Sept. 1722 Nicholas Anthony [*Boston Marriages* [**arrow left** to B in Boston Marriages][**F12**][**arrow right** to highlight title][**Control+F8**][**2**][**4**][**arrow left** to margin and **Tab** five times to indent], 104; identified only by name, she could [**arrow left** to margin and **Tab** five times to indent] have been the widow, or someone not related to Joseph[2] [**arrow left** once][**F12**][**arrow right** once][**Control+F8**][**1**][**1**][**arrow left** to margin and **Tab** five times to indent] Armington.[**Enter**]

[**Tab**][**Tab**]2.[**Tab**]ii.[**Tab**]Joseph, b. 1707; d. Rehoboth, Mass., 15 August 1746; m. there [**arrow left** to margin and **Tab** five times to indent] 27 May 1729 Hannah[4][**arrow left** once][**F12**][**arrow right** once][**1**][**1**] Chaffee.[**Enter**]

[**Enter**]

[**Tab**]2.   JOSEPH[2] ARMINGTON [treat name and generation number in same fashion as JOSEPH[1] ARMINGTON, above], born on the English Channel island of Guernsey, in 1707 [*Americana*[highlight title and [**Control+F8**][**2**][**4**]], 14:169], died in Rehoboth, Massachusetts, 15 August 1746, during an epidemic.[**Enter**]

[**Tab**]He was married by the Reverend David Turner in Rehoboth, 27 May 1729, to HANNAH[4] CHAFFEE* [*Rehoboth VR*[italicize same as source in previous paragraph], 2:142], who died there 22 Feb. 1799 [4:219].[**Enter**]

[**Tab**]He was a brickmaker.[**Enter**]

[**Tab**]Children, born in Rehoboth [2:107]:[**Enter**]

[**Tab** three times]i.[**Tab**]Nicholas[3][highlight or block and then super-script the digit], b. 12 Jan. 1729/30; d. there 28 Jan. 1729/30

[1:242].[**arrow left** to margin and **Tab** five times to indent][**Enter**]
[**Tab** three times]ii.[**Tab**]Joseph, b. 4 June 1731; d. 27 April 1817 ["Marriages and Death," *NEHGR*, 22:354]; m. (int. Rehoboth 19 April 1760) Esther Walker.[move cursor and use **F12** to block NEHGR, then use **Control+F8** and [2][4] to *italicize* source][move cursor to left margin(s) as necessary and **Tab** as necessary to set left margins][**Enter**]
[**Tab** three times]iii.[**Tab**]Josiah, b. 28 July 1733; d. there 13 May 1736 [2:243].[**Enter**]
[**Tab** twice to decimal tab and type while seeing digit move to left]3.[**Tab**]iv.[**Tab**]John, b. 12 June 1735; d. Waterford, Vermont; m. (1) 11 Jan. 1757 Ruth[4] Kent, m. (2) Chloe Newman.[**Enter**]
[**Tab** three times]v.[**Tab**]Deliverance, b. 24 Oct. 1737; d. there 28 August 1746 [2:254][**Enter**, and continue to work format with:]

vi.   Susannah, b. 9 Jan. 1739/40; d. there 28 August 1746 [2: 254].[Note that to break the source entry it was only necessary to leave a space after the colon.]

vii. Hannah, b. 20 April 1742; int. Rehoboth 12 Feb. 1763 Thomas McClish [3:343].

viii. Josiah, b. 4 April 1744; m. there 18 Nov. 1765 Ruth Bowen [3:343].

ix.   William, b. 22 Nov. 1746.

3.   JOHN[3] ARMINGTON, born in Rehoboth, Massachusetts, 12 June 1735, has been said to have died in Waterford, Vermont, but no probate file has been found for him there.

He married first, 11 Jan. 1757, RUTH[4] KENT*, and married second, according to intentions of marriage published in Rehoboth, 13 Jan. 1788, Chloe Newman of Rehoboth.[Note that only the name of the ancestral wife is given in upper case].

He appeared on the sixth list of Rehoboth taxpayers on 5 Nov. 1759, but was assessed no tax [Bowen, 4:95]. Ten years later he owned no real property but was assessed [**Control+v**]4,11(£ sign)[**Enter**]4.4s on personal property [Bowen 4:111]. In later years he moved to Waterford, Vermont.

Children, by first wife, born in Rehoboth [3:77]:

i.   Sylvester[4], b. 20 Nov. 1757; d. there 7 March 1758 [3:359].

ii.   Joseph, b. 12 Feb. 1759.

iii. Molly, b. 13 Oct. 1760.

iv.   Hannah, b. 20 Jan. 1764.

v.   Bety, b. 23 Sept. 1765.

vi.   Russell, b. 16 April 1759.

*   vii. Ruth, b. 29 June 1771; m. Barrington, R.I., 5 August 1790;

Enoch[6] Remington.
viii.   Olive, b. 16 August 1773; m. Rehoboth [3:313] 6 Oct. 1791
         James Peck.
 ix.   John, b. 10 May 1776.
  x.   Prudence, b. 14 August 1778; m. Rehoboth [3:315] 19 Nov.
         1798 Oliver Chaffee.
Child, by second wife, born in Rehoboth [3:77]:
 xi.   Abigail, b. 18 March 1789.

§ § §

MANUEL SETTING OF PAGES HEADINGS

While pages headings are general set automatically as a part of the computer format process, once the information has been entered, it is a simple matter to type them individually. The right hand, odd numbered pages, can be typed as follows:
[Shift+F6]APPENDIX[Alt+F6]155[Enter][Enter]. This will read:
APPENDIX   155

The left hand, even numbered pages, can be typed:
156[Shift+F6]HOW TO PUBLISH YOUR FAMILY HISTORY[Enter]
[Enter]. This will read:
156   HOW TO PUBLISH YOUR FAMILY HISTORY

Notice that there should be a line of space following the heading.

§ § §

USING MACROS TO AVOID REPETITIVE TASKS

I do not claim to be an expert at using computers. I have used only two, both IBM compatible, and two word processing programs. It seems necessary to point out that when first learning a program it is a good idea to read the entire manual, absorb the basic skills of using the program, and then, after a few weeks, read the manual again. This allows the user to recognize features available in the program which can be extremely useful. A few months later a third reading can be very rewarding.

One of the great features of WordPerfect®, and many other programs, is the Macro. For example, if you are entering the ancestral string of names after ten people in a genealogy, all of whom have the same ancestral line for ten generations, with a generation number after each name, it is not only unnecessary to repeatedly type in all the names and commands, but it is foolhardy, for a carefully checked macro can do it right every time. Further, a macro can be changed after using one string so it does not become necessary to create completely new macros with new names.

Dr. Stanley Richard Ames' *How to Write and Publish Your Family History Using WordPerfect*® has proved very helpful, and is available from the publisher, Heart of the Lakes Publishing, P. O. Box 299, Interlaken, NY 14847-0299 at $19.20 postpaid. New York residents must add sales tax. Macros are discussed with great clarity on pages 61-68.

Regrettably, the rest of the volume is somewhat dated, it having been published in 1988, before it became practical for the average genealogist to consider using a LaserJet printer. It shows how to print to dot matrix, and does not deal with the questions of proportionally spaced lettering and right hand justification, treated above.

§ § §

INDEX